EDUCATORS' FEEDI

Bright Ribbons is a work of art. Lotus Howard's years of love and appreciation for children, her joy for teaching and learning, her creativity and the results of her quest for the best, most successful and fulfilling practices are woven throughout. Every child who crossed her door and every colleague who shared her journey were blessed to have known her. This book is a gift to all who open it.

—Dian Pomeranz, Teacher
Hartford, CT

There are so many wonderful ideas and strategies in *Bright Ribbons* for working with children from 'many' cultures. This book would be a wonderful resource in every classroom and I would recommend it to anyone who works with children from different cultural backgrounds.

—Susan Sleswick, Teacher
Traralgon, Victoria, Australia

Lotus Howard was definitely one of those creative teachers doing whatever was necessary and needed to make sure her students learned while simultaneously honoring them as cultural beings.

—Victoria Romero, Principal, Educational Consultant
Seattle, WA

I loved *Bright Ribbons*! I loved the examples that could be easily adapted to almost any teaching style. It wasn't overwhelming or an "add on." A busy teacher with an interest in making some changes could start out immediately with small changes. This book MUST be taught at the university level...not as an elective!

—Susan Hopkins, Teacher
Albuquerque, NM

I am completely impressed and thrilled that teachers will have access to such a wonderful resource!

—Pam Bridges, Educational Consultant & Advocate
Bridges to Educational Resources
Lakewood, WA
pamandparis@gmail.com

Bright Ribbons

For my precious grandchildren, Orion, Mihna, and Chelan,
And all the children of the next seven generations

Bright Ribbons

*Weaving Culturally Responsive Teaching
Into the Elementary Classroom*

Lotus Linton Howard

Foreword by Gary Howard

CORWIN
A SAGE Publishing Company

FOR INFORMATION:

Corwin

A SAGE Company

2455 Teller Road

Thousand Oaks, California 91320

(800) 233-9936

www.corwin.com

SAGE Publications Ltd.

1 Oliver's Yard

55 City Road

London, EC1Y 1SP

United Kingdom

SAGE Publications India Pvt. Ltd.

B 1/I 1 Mohan Cooperative Industrial Area

Mathura Road, New Delhi 110 044

India

SAGE Publications Asia-Pacific Pte. Ltd.

3 Church Street

#10-04 Samsung Hub

Singapore 049483

Program Director: Dan Alpert

Senior Associate Editor: Kimberly
    Greenberg

Editorial Assistant: Katie Crilley

Production Editor: Amy Schroller

Copy Editor: Beth Ginter

Typesetter: Hurix Systems Pvt. Ltd.

Proofreader: Penelope Sippel

Indexer: Rick Hurd

Cover Designer: Alexa Turner

Marketing Manager: Charline Maher

Printed in the United States of America

ISBN 978-1-5063-2525-5

This book is printed on acid-free paper.

SFI Certified Sourcing
www.sfiprogram.org
SFI-00453

16 17 18 19 20 10 9 8 7 6 5 4 3 2 1

Contents

Foreword

Lotus began her teaching career in an inner-city school in 1968. Her first-grade classroom served primarily low-income African American, Puerto Rican, Italian, and Irish kids from the neighborhood public housing projects. This was a time before words like multicultural education, differentiation, learning styles, and cooperative learning had become a normal part of the educational lexicon. But somehow Lotus understood that her central order of business as a white teacher in this setting was to form positive relationships with her kids, and her students definitely got it that she enjoyed and respected them. She talked openly about cultural differences, brought all kinds of diverse ethnic content into her lessons, and worked constantly to bolster her students' self-esteem and to honor their different ways of learning. She was a culturally responsive teacher before the term was invented.

By October of that first year, the word was out among the kids that Ms. Howard's room in the basement was the place to hang out during lunch and before and after school. Kids of various ages liked to come in to talk and help her, and when I would stop by to pick her up at the end of the day, it was apparent that the kids felt comfortable, respected, seen, and safe in her presence. Sadly, some of the other adults in the building didn't have the same desire to connect with the kids. Her principal even told her at one point to stop letting the older students come into her room: "They'll just cause problems and take advantage." Lotus learned early on that being an advocate for marginalized kids sometimes requires us to resist the negative stereotypes of other adults in our schools.

Since these early experiences, Lotus has taught all grades K through 6 in many different settings. Focusing on cultural differences, diverse learning styles, and each child's individual uniqueness has always been central to her work.

When I lead my culturally responsive teaching workshops with educators throughout the country, I always tell stories about Lotus's elementary classroom and her strategies for teaching across differences. In one session in Minnesota, I was waxing so eloquent with stories about Lotus's teaching that the Pre–K and elementary folks lobbied their district supervisor after the session, "We like Gary's work, but since most of his primary and elementary examples come from his wife, can't we just bring in Lotus next time?"

That request and Lotus's subsequent work with teachers throughout the country eventually led to the creation of this book. I asked Lotus if she would take some time to share with other educators her insights, her wisdom, her strategies, and most of all, her spirit of inclusive, imaginative, and powerful teaching. *Bright Ribbons* resulted from that request and now comes to you as a practical guide for culturally responsive teaching in the elementary classroom, written by one of the best teachers I have ever known.

I am excited about this book and so happy that Corwin has made it possible to share Lotus's insights with you. *Bright Ribbons* is not a formula, and it's certainly not a scripted curriculum. If it were either of these, then it would not be worthy of the complexity and importance of our work. This inspirational and down-to-earth book transcends the current test-driven craziness and reminds us what it really means to be a committed and visionary teacher. It speaks to the best in each of us, and it honors you and your professionalism. I welcome you to the many *Bright Ribbons* that are woven together throughout these pages, and I thank you for the good work you do every day in your classroom for the sake of our nation's richly diverse children.

Gary Howard, Author
We Can't Teach What We Don't Know:
White Teachers/Multiracial Schools
We Can't Lead Where We Won't Go: An Educator's Guide to Equity

Preface

My teaching career, spanning four decades, has been a smorgasbord of educational environments. During these years, much good research and numerous theoretical and persuasive books that describe the urgent need for "multicultural" and "culturally responsive" pedagogies and curricula have arisen. I am thankful for these founding fathers and mothers of the movement for equity in education who have laid crucial groundwork. And I am also grateful for those who continue to refine and polish our understanding of what equitable education requires through their research and observations of children. You will find many of these respected names referenced throughout this book. In addition, there has been a vast proliferation of multicultural literature for children that became available in the last 40 years, much of which is offered in the Resources sections of *Bright Ribbons*.

However, in spite of a plethora of multicultural books, I wanted to take the excellent research, the requisite theory and rationale, and the good children's literature to the next step. I needed ways to more thoroughly address the issues and needs of the broad range of culturally diverse students under my influence. My questions have been these: What do I do in the classroom? How do I apply all this important information on a daily basis? I wanted practical materials, processes, and activities to help me bring greater Culturally Responsive Teaching (CRT) knowledge and deeper ideals and ideas into a comprehensive approach with the elementary school children I taught—methodologies beyond the all-too prevalent and superficial kind of practice that only focuses on cultural folklore, artifacts, and celebrations. I wanted to develop a way of teaching that would permeate and unify the entire educational experience, all day, every day. Teaching in such a variety of cultural settings, it was my growing passion for social justice and the educational rights of all children, as well as a commitment to develop the skills of global citizenship, that motivated me to continually seek and develop this kind of curriculum.

I found that the whole process of good CRT had to begin with me. As I developed greater self-reflective skills and knowledge about myself and the conditioning of my own cultural background. I learned how many of my assumptions about children and schooling were due to unexamined cultural biases. By teaching in much the same way as I was taught, I discovered that in many ways, I was perpetuating racism and inequity without realizing it. Thus, I began a long process of educational "awakening." As I became more open to learning from my students and their cultures, I grew more appreciative of their many diversities, more knowledgeable about how they learn, and more aware of how I can either be in the way of, or supportive of that. This "awakening" process, I discovered, never ends. I am awakening still. As much as this book is a compendium of ideas, activities, and inspirations, *Bright Ribbons* is also an invitation for your own self-reflection as you explore new avenues for accessing and developing the intelligence and success of your students.

This book is designed to help beginning as well as seasoned teachers, in both preservice and inservice courses, to make Culturally Responsive Teaching integral to their practice. The activities and approaches presented in this book are those that have proven most beneficial for me in teaching a broad panoply of ethnically, racially, and culturally diverse students. While these methods are essential in the movement toward greater inclusion and narrowing of "achievement gaps," it is also my belief that *all* children, even those who are well-groomed for school success, benefit from a CRT approach. Such an approach incorporates a variety of learning modalities, many of which are common to other-than-Western cultures—modalities that markedly augment learning for everyone. In addition, a comprehensive approach to Culturally Responsive Teaching allows all students to gain the social and educational survival skills of deeper self-respect, coupled with tolerance, acceptance, appreciation, enjoyment, and even admiration for those who are different from them. This is the kind of global citizen I believe we, as educators, are responsible to produce. With these CRT methods coupled with deep reflection, I and my students grew more confident, happier, and more able to relate authentically to each other, which created a warm environment for students to thrive academically. We all became better learners and better people for having touched each others' lives with the increasing respect and love that is at the heart of Culturally Responsive Teaching. I offer you these strategies as ways and means for going deeper and becoming more authentic as a learner in your own right and "awakening" into a highly proficient, culturally responsive teacher.

Acknowledgments

I want to thank many wonderful people for their support during the various stages of this book, my friends of various ethnicities and educational roles—David Koyama, Susan Hopkins, and Dian Pomeranz—who have conscientiously reviewed these pages and added marvelous suggestions. I thank Ian and Sheila Whitehead and Sharon Hartnett who put the manuscript in the hands of other helpful critics. And I particularly want to thank Victoria Romero who took so much time to meticulously comb through the pages and offer innumerable changes and additions to the text. To all of you I owe my gratitude and respect for the critique, the support, and the encouragement you have given me. I thank you deeply.

This book could not have been born without the suggestions and abiding personal and professional support of my dear, beloved partner. Gary not only convinced me of the need for the book but painstakingly edited every chapter . . . several times! He presents my work with pride to his colleagues and clients in the field. Thank you for believing in me, Gary.

And I owe much to our grown children, Benjie and Reya, who were two of my students in our little one-room schoolhouse in a country town. I thank you for teaching me to teach and for growing up to be such beautiful human beings. I thank you for your constant love and support. I especially thank you and your beautiful partners, Naomi and Makéta, for making me a grandmother. You have brought Orion, Mihna, and Chelan into this world and are doing a fine job of parenting these precious ones! My prayers are being answered as their teachers are following suit and honoring them for their own beautiful, unique ways of being.

PUBLISHER'S ACKNOWLEDGMENTS

Corwin would gratefully like to thank the following reviewers for their contributions:

Melanie S. Hedges
Art Teacher, NBCT
West Gate Elementary School
West Palm Beach, FL

Gayla LeMay
ESOL Lead Teacher
Louise Radloff Middle School
Duluth, GA

Dr. Toni B. Ramey
Middle School Science Teacher
Mobile County Public School System
Mobile, AL

About the Author

 **Lotus Linton Howard, PhD,** has taught in a variety of elementary school settings, including public, private, inner city, small town, rural, and reservation schools. She created and taught for several years in a one-room country school, Grades 1–8. Over 40 years of teaching, she has worked with children and adults from very diverse cultural backgrounds and has observed, firsthand, how culture influences one's perceptions, cognition, communication, and attitudes.

Lotus taught preservice Multicultural Education courses at Seattle Pacific University and has presented at a variety of state and national conferences. She was also on the curriculum development team for the REACH Center for Multicultural Education, developing sample lesson plans that could be infused into the normal curriculum at each grade level, and are now being used internationally. Collaborating with the REACH Center, Lotus enlisted the cooperation of Native American elders and educators to create a course through Western Washington University, "The Indian Child in the Classroom," to demonstrate how intelligence is developed, accessed, and appraised differently in Native communities. Lotus has offered culturally responsive inservice training for elementary teachers in numerous states.

Lotus has also had extensive global experience observing cultures in 21 countries, studying educational practices, and learning about and from cultures outside our U.S. borders. Her PhD thesis, entitled *Remembering the Circle*, is based on the commonalities of a variety of indigenous cultures and their continuing contributions to the emerging global community.

Lotus received her BS degree in Early Childhood Education at Southern Connecticut State University, 5th Year Research and Training in Orff Schulwerk Music Instruction and Waldorf Schools through Western Washington University, and her PhD in Transformational Education from Union Institute of Ohio.

Lotus lives in Seattle with her husband, Gary Howard. Their two grown children, along with their partners and three amazing multiracial and multicultural grandchildren, live nearby.

Stringing the Vertical Threads

1

Basic Beliefs Underlying
Culturally Responsive Teaching

B efore beginning her work, the weaver must first secure vertical threads onto the loom. This is the "warp" through which the "woof" of pattern and color will be woven horizontally. Similarly, as we approach our loom of Culturally Responsive Teaching (CRT), it is important and helpful to address some basic beliefs about ourselves and our students, and about the deeper purpose of education. These are the foundational premises throughout this book that provide a strong warp for the cloth we will weave, the distinctive texture of thought and belief underlying the very best of Culturally Responsive Teaching.

These basic precepts belong to the realm of one's deepest convictions about life and learning. The warp of our individual beliefs is the foundation of our attitudes and actions in the classroom. Therefore, it is essential to examine our perspectives and perceptions to see where change might be necessary or new understanding acquired.

Some of the tenets presented here have been adapted from the materials created by the REACH Center for Multicultural Education (www.reachctr.org/), developed there by my husband, Gary, and other REACH trainers. Other precepts have grown out of many years of my own research and engagement in the fundaments of successful teaching. These precepts comprise a philosophical foundation that will support you in becoming an effective culturally responsive teacher.

If any of these foundational ideas are not yet your own, I ask that you allow yourself to "try them on" to see if they might make your teaching practice richer and more rewarding and your students' experiences more enlivened and productive. Following are the 10 Vertical Threads onto which we will later weave the Seven Principles for CRT.

1. Relationship Is the Foundation of Good Teaching and Learning

All learning is based on our relationships. Relationship is the essence of education, and from the influences of our first relationships, we pattern our approach to life. In his workshops with teachers, Gary Howard says, "Relationship *matters.*" And he defines cultural competence as "the will and the ability to form authentic and effective relationships across differences" (Howard, 2015). We know from stereotype-threat research that intellectual performance is dependent on students' feelings of belonging and their trust in the people around them (Aaronson & Steel, 2005). Good teacher-student relationships are at the heart of students' attitudes toward learning and their abilities to receive, process, and retain information. Our relationships with our students in the classroom today not only affect their achievement in the moment and in the year they are in our care but continue to influence them in their feelings toward school and education for years to come.

As we all know, not all children come to school emotionally prepared for the rigors of learning. Not all children are given the experience of being truly seen, known, respected, and cared about. Not all children are given the unconditional regard that is at the heart of healthy human development. Because of this, there is a compensatory role good teachers must play in the lives of many children—children across all racial, cultural, and economic lines—who need relationships with loving adults in their lives. Yet regardless of what they are getting or not getting at home, *all* children learn best through strong relationships with their teachers.

The first task of a good teacher is to consciously and deliberately establish this essential ground of quality relationship with every child. The tone of trust and mutual respect upon which the reciprocal door of teaching and learning swings is perhaps our most important pedagogical tool as culturally responsive teachers.

2. The Teacher Is a Lifelong Learner

It is liberating for us as teachers to consciously acknowledge that life is a constant process of learning. It takes us off the hook of needing to be "right" all the time—an assumption I find teachers often adopt as a function of our profession. The pressure to be the one "in-the-know" about all things comes from the philosophical model that views children as empty vessels needing to be filled up with the knowledge of the world, doled out by our adult expertise.

If we can accept a more realistic role as guides and mentors for young people who are already quite full of innate intelligence and giftedness, then our job becomes more enjoyable and more authentic. Although we teachers are intelligent and educated adults who *do* know a great deal, we are, at the same time, ignorant of many things. By admitting this from time to time to our students, we establish a ground of honesty and humility that they will deeply respect. Rather than trying to be the *source* of all-important information (which no one individual could ever embody), we free ourselves to explore many answers together with our students. We become the guides for how and where to find the information they seek and enthusiastic role models for the lifelong love of learning that we want to engender in them.

We model this by being open with our students about things we may be learning outside the classroom as well as inside. When we talk to our students about our hobbies, our classes, our travels, or other experiences we are passionate about, we are enthusiastic role models for a lifelong love of learning. When we share with them something we learned from a friend, or from one of the students in our classroom, we demonstrate there is something to be learned in every moment and every situation.

Occasionally we can let our students see us deliberating about a negative encounter we might have had and what we should do about it. We can elicit their suggestions. It is important to be selective about what we share with our students. But by appropriately modeling our own problem-solving process in everyday situations, we can help our students realize that every struggle in their lives has potential personal growth hidden within it.

Contrary to what might be feared as loss of respect or classroom control if we share any uncertainty with our students, the opposite is usually the case. We can still be trusted authorities in their lives without needing to "know it all." We can remain firm and maintain high expectations while at the same time reveal our vulnerability. Children respect honesty more than "perfection," and they will eagerly join with us in a mutual pursuit of knowledge. Allowing ourselves to be honest about what we do not know teaches children that ignorance about something is not a failure, but a stimulus for finding answers, acquiring more information, and gaining greater awareness. The ability to genuinely say, "I don't know, but let's find out," will take us far. We find that our students' respect for us grows in direct proportion to our honesty with them.

This becomes most noticeably beneficial when we open ourselves to learning about our students' cultural backgrounds. Our active interest and readiness to learn about the many different cultural patterns, practices, and perspectives of our students and their families offers them valuable opportunities to teach us something, to share who they really are, and to feel appreciated for their cultural knowledge and expertise.

3. Context Is as Important as Content

The mastery of Culturally Responsive Teaching requires a keen awareness of the contextual ambiance of the classroom and an appreciation of its importance to the learning experience. Many children have "field-sensitive" ways of perceiving and learning. That is, they are holistically oriented and constantly attuned to every nuance in the atmosphere of their environment. The emotional tone of the teacher, displayed by our attitudes, preferences, values, and "voice," is immediately picked up by the sensitive antennae of children. Attending to the contextual background of the educational process is sometimes referred to as being aware of the "hidden curriculum" (Glossary of Education Reform, 2015) that directly affects each student's degree of concentration and ability to absorb intellectual content.

As culturally responsive teachers, we consciously and consistently recognize this field-sensitivity in our teaching design and classroom organization. We pay close attention to the messages we send to children through body language, tone of voice, and choice of words and behavior. This requires continual self-observance and self-reflection.

The social-emotional context of learning imparts its own lessons and enhances the successful mental/conceptual learning of the "explicit" curriculum made up of the objectives and content at each grade level. Many of the suggestions provided in these *Bright Ribbons* chapters relate more to context than to content and are intended to support the establishment of a rich and inviting backdrop that will enhance and enliven the overall drama of learning in your classroom.

4. Everything Can Be Seen From Multiple Perspectives

In left-brain dominant educational models, people are trained to believe that there is only one right answer for any question. Things are perceived from a dualistic perspective of right or wrong, good or bad. When this is the case, all other answers or points of view are deemed incorrect or mistaken (sometimes even considered evil or dangerous), and people will go to great lengths to defend their sense of rightness, sometimes against all reason. This bias toward bifurcation reaches deeply into the subconscious, dampening creativity, reducing the exploration of alternative possibilities, and rendering us defensive and inflexible for fear of being *wrong*. Such an impulse also creates the predisposition to judge others for their differences, claiming "If I am right, then he must be wrong."

More right-brain and holistic cultures and educational environments, on the other hand, teach children that there are always multiple possibilities in an unlimited universe and numerous answers to any challenge. Through our exposure to other cultural ways of thinking, perceiving, and behaving, we all have much to learn. This simple yet basic premise of multiple perspectives breeds tolerance, acceptance, and openness. When we as teachers reinforce the idea that there are many ways to solve a problem or look at a situation, we are helping to infuse the left-brain intellect with right-brain openness and creativity, seeding the capacity for healthy cultural responsiveness and wisdom in our students.

This higher order thinking skill—the ability to see more than one point of view—lies at the heart of Culturally Responsive Teaching. It is an urgently needed prerequisite for global citizenship. It is the ability to entertain multiple perspectives on any question or topic that allows the perceiver to hold two competing opinions in mind at one time, thus opening the possibility for considering the worth of each point of view. This does not require that we always agree with another opinion, but only that we learn to give time for thoughtful consideration of alternative ideas. This stance engenders respect not only for someone else's perspective on a specific subject but for the experiences and the world view from which that other perspective was born. As Einstein so aptly modeled in his presentation of the Theory of Relativity, reality is constructed differently when viewed through various lenses. The culturally responsive teacher allows for different windows on "truth."

The capacity for multiple perspectives allows us and our students to embrace ambiguity and to actually enjoy viewing diverse aspects of any picture. It is an inclusive way of being, a "both/and" way of looking at life. The need to be overly definitive or exclusively right gives way to modest and friendly dialogue with those who see the world through a different lens, recognizing that no one viewpoint can possibly grasp the entire tapestry of existence. Embracing multiple perspectives is an acknowledgement that we are each enhanced through conversation and connection across our differences. This flexible outlook does not limit our capacity to form opinions and have our own beliefs, but it allows us to hold those opinions lightly enough to keep our beliefs open to maturation and ever-evolving understanding. It also allows us to laugh at ourselves, to take a second look at our beliefs when we become too serious, too self-righteous, or more married to opinion and belief than to love.

By expanding our capacity to consider multiple perspectives, we model for our students a humble, generous, and inclusive way of being. Watching us, they discover there are many levels of truth, countless ways to perceive reality, numerous ideas to consider, and scores of ways to express even one idea. The world is a bigger place when we can think this way. By becoming more inclusive and magnanimous in their thinking and feeling, our students gain respect for both themselves and others. An open heart and an open mind are essential elements of CRT. Throughout this book, we will utilize the concept of multiple perspectives as an open-minded, open-hearted way of approaching learning and life.

5. The Classroom Is a Community

With so much divisiveness and alienation in the world today, the basic skills related to community-building are a critical and healing part of Culturally Responsive Teaching. The dominant paradigms of individuality and superiority over others that foster exclusivity, competition, and survival-of-the-fittest do not engender the creation of sustainable and healthy communities. The plethora of cliques in our schools and gangs on our streets indicates that our young people are hungry for community. But such quasi-communities do not really alleviate the loneliness and self-absorption of their members, based as they are on groupthink and expectations of sameness within the circle, combined with judgment of, or hatred for, those outside the circle. Cliques and gangs are the youthful mirrors of the prevailing pain that characterizes much of the larger adult society.

Genuine community, on the other hand, fosters both self-respect and authentic respect for others. Since children's natural predisposition for connection is easily thwarted in individualistic, competitive environments, community-building must be intentionally included as part of the classroom ethos. When an authentic and cooperative learning community is established, a sense of safety for one's own personhood is secured. Shared ideas with others are engendered. Reciprocity is enhanced. Communication skills are emphasized and constantly reinforced. Children are taught the skills for conflict resolution. Speaking one's truth and maintaining one's boundaries are clear expectations as is respecting those rights in others. Individual uniqueness is valued. Each student's viewpoint is welcomed and encouraged. Harmony, cooperation, and respect are intentionally reinforced. Commonalities, as well as differences, are acknowledged and appreciated. In healthy community, the students experience the power of their interdependent giftedness as learners. Since many of our students may be coming to us from cultures where community and cooperation are deeply valued, they have much to teach us about building a positive learning community. When community is established in our classrooms, there is more room for the creative synergy that fashions a dynamic learning context for all.

6. We Are All Alike and We Are All Different

Culturally responsive teachers offer a balanced perspective that appreciates our unique personal and cultural differences, while at the same time values our fundamental unity as members of the human family. This balanced perspective positively permeates the learning atmosphere of the classroom. If we focus only on differences or only on sameness, we do not sufficiently serve our students. Both are mutual, interdependent aspects of a healthy outlook toward oneself and others. To exclusively emphasize the sameness vector, *how we are alike*, focusing only on the unity aspect of our human nature, is to be "color blind" to a student's distinctive identity. There are teachers who, in trying to be equitable with their students, sometimes claim, "I don't see color." However, if one asks people of color how that statement makes them feel, they will usually say that they do not feel seen for who they are. "Color blindness" deprives us of the beauty, depth, and stimulation of diversity. On the other hand, to solely focus on *how we are different* (even when differences are valued) can cause us to miss out on the warmth of connection that comes from our kinship and community as human beings.

A "both/and" approach to similarities and differences is a central quality of Culturally Responsive Teaching. "How are these alike?" and "How are they different?" are compare-and-contrast questions that help students develop social skills as well as the capacity for higher level thinking that leads to gains in academic achievement (Marzano, 2007). The frequent use of compare-and-contrast questions will be demonstrated in several subject areas throughout this book. Providing a dynamic balance of sameness and difference is a foundational premise that makes education more substantial and life more interesting.

7. We Are All American Plus

One of the most important metaphors for a CRT teacher to adopt is the image of our country as a "salad bowl," with an array of amazingly diverse fruits and vegetables tossed into it. The outmoded "melting pot" theory suggests that people must get hurled into a hot pot and then melted down into some homogenous mixture that is accepted as "American." In contrast, the salad bowl symbolism allows us to keep our personal, ethnic, and cultural identities intact and still be flavored with a dressing that unifies us in our American-ness. As such, everyone and every culture are welcomed and considered valuable to the social fabric. Unless we are Native American, every member of this society has roots in another land, and each culture that has arrived here has brought its contributions and its struggles to the emerging civilization.

In my lifetime career with children and teachers in the field of Multi-cultural Education, I have observed that many white teachers, especially those who have grown up in predominantly white communities, have a tendency to see others, especially people of color, as the ones having culture and racial identity and fail to see the cultural milieu in which they themselves swim. Yet our students are very aware of our cultural distinctiveness. The term "white" is a generalized descriptive adjective that includes a gestalt of numerous attitudes, beliefs, and behaviors that are noticed by many non-white students. Greater awareness of how we are each influenced and formed by our cultural environments and the ability to appreciate, as well as critique, our own unique cultural heritage are big self-reflective steps for teachers toward greater CRT expertise. *All* Americans have distinguishing cultural identities beneath that of being American.

Adopting the salad bowl viewpoint also significantly alters a common and usually unconscious paradigm that seeks sameness in others in order to feel they are "one of us." White people often have a subconscious tendency to perceive people of color, or those who come from cultures other than their own, as someone other than American, someone "forever foreign." It is a common complaint from young people of color who have been born in this country and have a mastery of the English language to still be frequently asked, "Where are you from?" And even Native American students, who are here on their original homeland, are sometimes considered to be outsiders by those who now occupy their land. Additionally, those students whose families have not yet obtained citizenship are still here now, participating in the richly diverse American mix that makes up our nation. So it is important for us to understand these in-group/out-group dynamics and counter cultural bias in ourselves in order to be more inclusive of all our students.

It is also critical to recognize that most young people want very much to be perceived and accepted as American by their peers and their teachers. So, while we are opening the doors for every child from any culture to feel welcome and at home in our classroom, it is important not to single out a child as a representative of, or spokesperson for, his culture—the "Exhibit A" phenomenon. It is optimum to allow our students to volunteer information about their linguistic and cultural heritage and all other groups with which they identify, in their own time, and by their own initiation, once they have determined that the environment in our classroom is culture-safe.

Furthermore, for those of us who teach in a situation where all our students are of one particular ethnic background, there are still many nuances of differences to honor among the individuals in our class. It is important to introduce our students to the extensive varieties of American groups in preparation for their exposure to more diversity later in their lives, even though those differences may not be present in our school. In this way, we are responsibly preparing them for informed participation in pluralistic American democracy and world citizenship.

8. Every Child Is Gifted

As demonstrated by Howard Gardner's analysis of eight kinds of intelligences (2011), giftedness is many-faceted. Stretching the screen even farther, we realize that giftedness is not limited to just eight facets but manifests in an infinite variety of forms. One child has a sense of humor that lights up the day. Another has the gift of compassion. Still others are dancers, artists, great debaters, or clever problem-solvers. Some are philosophers. Some are organizers or natural leaders. Some students are bursting with infectious enthusiasm. Others are able to be pensive, thoughtful, and deep. While it is true that children have varying levels of ability in the skills we teach, all children are gifted at something, and these gifts, if recognized and educed in the classroom environment, can greatly enhance the learning experience. Expanding our understanding of intelligence beyond the boundaries of standardized testing, we can see that all kids are smart in different ways. Out of respectful awareness of the precious giftedness of each student, relationships are enhanced and teaching becomes more supportive of success for every child.

Each one of us comes into this world with much to learn and also with much to give. When we feel our gifts are recognized and received by others, we become happier and more generous (Dixon, 2011). When we, as teachers, value and capitalize upon each student's inherent talents and gifts, we reinforce, again and again, her understanding that differences are respected in our presence, that everyone can contribute to the common good, and that each child is safe and appreciated for being exactly who she is in our classroom.

Broadening this notion of giftedness to include the many aspects of culture that children bring, our classroom becomes rich with giftedness and everyone benefits from not only realizing their own contributions to the collective but valuing those of others. Our students have the opportunity to see the world through a lens that is broader and more inclusive than the dominant linear and single-dimensional lens of the modern world that focuses too much on making judgments and creating hierarchies of worth.

By appreciating our students' individual and cultural gifts, we contribute to the transformational movement of Culturally Responsive Teaching that goes beyond the "one-size-fits-all," linear, singularly left-brain definition of what is good and valuable in society. Acknowledging the giftedness of each child, we and our students can enjoy the rich diversity within our classroom and capitalize on the multiple intelligences that everyone brings to the process.

9. Any Student Can Learn Anything

Given the right environment and the right approach, any child can learn almost anything. This belief may be difficult to adopt at first, for our experience tells us that people come into life with many levels of ability and intelligence—and they certainly do. Furthermore, our programming tells us, "You can't squeeze blood out of a turnip." But the questions are these: Who is the judge of these things? Who really knows who the turnips are? Do we have the right to make that pronouncement for any of our students? Many of the world's geniuses did very poorly in school.

Much of what children are capable of doing comes directly from the mirrors of themselves that the adults in their lives hold up. So does it not seem reasonable that we should be erring in the direction of having too great a belief in our students' abilities rather than creating a ceiling of limitation for them by our own potentially erroneous judgments? Starting with the conviction that any student can learn anything, we find that they do learn more often than they don't. Through our belief in their capacity to learn, we create a powerful magnetic field that draws them toward success. It is also essential, of course, to guard against being disappointed in our students when and if they do not measure up to our expectations. Disappointment can induce guilt and shame, so we must maintain our positive belief in their potential, offering encouragement all the way. Our job is to continually seek the keys that will unlock their intelligence. If the environment is conducive to learning, if we are loving to our students and respectful of their diverse backgrounds, if the material is presented in engaging and gradient stages, and if it is offered through a variety of modalities, then most often the learning will happen! And we see the fruits of our belief that given the right environment and the right approach, any child can learn almost anything (Blankstein & Noguera, 2015;

Chenowith, 2007). In the chapters that follow, we will see that effective CRT is undergirded by a strong belief in the intelligence and capability of our students.

10. Comprehensive Learning Addresses the Head, the Hands, and the Heart

Children are whole people with widely varying propensities and preferences for learning. The outcomes of our teaching are more remarkable, meaningful, and lasting when we approach our students through a range of portals that include thinking, feeling, and doing. Although many educators acknowledge the importance of these multiple doorways to learning, the current top-down mandates for scripted lessons and standardized outcomes have too often narrowed the way we teach. Teachers may often feel overwhelmed trying to comply with the many requirements and expectations of the job, too busy to study or apply what research tells us—that comprehensive learning requires a multisensory, emotionally rich, and academically inviting environment (Jensen, 2005).

However, teaching in a holistic and culturally responsive manner does not force us to pore too long over lesson plans or create more stress for ourselves. By focusing on the value of addressing the head, the heart, and the hands (or thinking, feeling, and doing) in the learning process, we can, in simple ways, make teaching much more pleasurable for ourselves and more effective for our students. Teaching any history lesson, for instance, can include a quick physical game and a reflective discussion about the emotional challenges of historical persons, as well as reading and summarizing content information. Approaching all skill development in this threefold way, we make the memory of the lesson more precise, more detailed, and more easily retrieved. Keeping the head, the hands, and the heart constantly in mind, we augment our lesson plans with varied and pleasurable challenges, without a lot of additional work on our part. In the chapters that follow, you will find many suggestions to support you in addressing the learning process in this multifaceted way.

With these Vertical Threads as the foundation of your professional approach, you are now ready to begin incorporating the Seven Principles of Culturally Responsive Teaching into your classroom practice. It is my sincere hope that these fundamental beliefs about teaching and learning will inspire your creative nature as a teacher and offer you a supportive warp onto which you can weave the bright ribbons of your own educational proficiency.

Red Ribbons 2

Teachers Are Personally
and Culturally Inviting

The climate for learning. . . cannot be separated from a climate
in which care, concern, and love are central.

—Sonia Nieto
Culturally Responsive Teaching Pioneer
University of Massachusetts

The journey through the many bright ribbons of Culturally Responsive Teaching should begin with you, the teacher. At the very heart of CRT is the child's relationship to you as a person. Because of children's natural trust in their teacher, your invitational style and appreciation for their uniqueness as individuals catalyzes their enthusiasm for learning. Of course, there are numerous other assets of a good CRT teacher—skills and attributes that we will address in the following chapters. Furthermore, I assume there are innumerable ways you are already personally inviting to your students. But your warmth and invitational style cannot be overemphasized as the first principle of CRT. The student's personal relationship with the teacher is fundamental to his experience of the safety and belonging required for effective information processing and school success (Hammond, 2015).

Remembering that each colored ribbon of the Seven Basic Principles of CRT will be woven through the framework of your philosophical belief system, it is vital to keep the Vertical Threads in mind as you proceed through the chapters. Your beliefs create your attitudes, which in turn produce your behaviors with your students. So it is fundamental to good CRT to continually examine your core beliefs and assumptions.

Although all of the Vertical Threads are interwoven and integral to each of the Seven Basic Principles, I suggest, for the sake of practice in growing your culturally responsive competence, that you try to relate the Red Ribbons focus around two specific Vertical Threads:

- **Relationship Is the Foundation of Good Teaching and Learning**
  and
- **The Teacher Is a Lifelong Learner**

Core beliefs and unexamined assumptions have much to do with how we were raised and educated. Do you, for instance, feel most comfortable teaching with a writing board behind you, a desk in front of you, and a somewhat distant relationship with your students because that is the way you were taught? Do you feel awkward, uncomfortable, or resistant to children who have a different cultural, racial, or sexual identity than you do? Do you love learning about new things both within the classroom and in your life? Do your students have opportunities to observe your continuing interest in learning and growing? Are you open with your students about your own interests? And are you truly interested in learning about *them*?

A great teacher of mine once told me that everyone is only partially baked. She said we will never be fully cooked because living is always about change, growth, and maturing wisdom. We are able to modify core beliefs when we take them out of the subconscious storage chest to dust off and look over with a critical eye. The more we are aware and conscious of our basic patterning, the more we have the power to alter what we want to change and keep what we feel is worth saving. In this way, we make the best choices for ourselves and our students in the light of a new day.

So return to the previous chapter, "Stringing the Vertical Threads." Think about your beliefs regarding these two statements: **Relationship Is the Foundation of Good Teaching and Learning**, and **The Teacher Is a Lifelong Learner**. Be honest with yourself. Look deeply into the beliefs you hold on these two subjects. Write them down. Then consider what beliefs need mending, updating, or remaking. What needs laundering? What needs tossing altogether? As you read further in this chapter, allow the Red Ribbons, regarding the personhood of the teacher, to weave themselves around and through your beliefs about relationship and giftedness. Be willing to update your beliefs in the light of new information or ideas.

The following suggestions, in the three categories of *Personal Connections, Teacher as Model*, and *Self-Reflective Teaching Style*, are offered to help you become even more aware of the verbal and nonverbal messages you give to your students through what you say and do in their presence.

PERSONAL CONNECTIONS

The way you begin and end each day's cycle and personally connect with your students throughout the day has much to do with how welcome and comfortable they feel in your classroom. It is crucial that you give time and attention to creating the positive tone in your classroom that will enhance learning for everyone. It is most important that you are authentic and true to your personal style and nature. You can have a gregarious, high-energy, vivid personality; a soft-spoken, gentle, and calm temperament; or a myriad of combinations of countless other characteristics. Like our students, we are all so beautifully different! But, to perform optimally, your students need to see you as their learning ally in the ways you respect, validate, and show deep interest in them.

You can enhance your personal warmth and invitational style in several ways:

Sample Personal Connections

Welcome at the Door

Jack, a fifth-grade teacher, was a bright model of inclusive CRT. I saw him standing at the door of his classroom every morning greeting each student with affection and respect. "Hola," he would say for "hello" on a particular week, or "Namaste," on another. As he greeted the students, he would often make inquiries about a baby coming in the family, or note a new pair of earrings, or mention a student's upcoming birthday. The days went fast in my friend's classroom of abundant learning activities, and I remember him often going overtime, with his students rushing out the door to catch the bus. But he tried to make a point to again stand at the doorway saying "good-bye" to them in the language of the morning greeting.

You too can welcome the children to school in the morning and send them home in the afternoon with your presence at the doorway and a personalized comment, a warm smile, and eye contact. This is a visceral message to your students that you care for them.

Many Ways to Say Hello and Good-Bye

Each week, teach the children, or have them teach you, a way of saying "hello" and "good-bye" in a new language.
    Practice using these greetings with your students for a week. Use words that come from languages

See RED RIBBONS RESOURCES: Personal Connections: Many Ways to Say Hello and Good-Bye.

(Continued)

(Continued)

both represented and not represented by the students in your class. Ask, "Who knows how to say 'hello' or 'good-bye' in another language?" Allow the students to volunteer information without singling anyone out as the model of their culture (what I call the "Exhibit A" phenomenon). Even if your main responsibility is to teach English mastery, you can certainly learn a few words in their languages to convey your interest in and enthusiasm about the diversity of language in the world. This powerful message to the children is twofold: (1) Their age-mates in the classroom and in other parts of the country and world greet others saying these words, and (2) All languages have value. Such a message helps the students go beyond inferior/superior thinking to the higher level thinking capacity for multiple perspectives (Howard, 2015). Hearing questions like this, they quickly learn that differences are not only accepted here but are valued; that their own language is appreciated; and that they, themselves, are safe in this place. This very simple activity serves not only to allow students to respect themselves and their own cultural background but to begin to be respectfully curious about others' differences as well.

Appreciation

Each day acknowledge every child with a comment of genuine interest, encouragement, and appreciation for her as a special person, as a successful learner, or as a valued member of the class community, taking care to be truthful and thoughtful in your feedback (Steele & Cohn-Vargas, 2013). Because a positive relationship with the teacher has one of the higher effect sizes for school success (Hattie, 2009), it behooves you to intentionally and genuinely capitalize on this dynamic as often as possible with your gifts of attention and acknowledgment for each child.

Correct Name Pronunciation

First graders in Minnesota were asked what made them feel like a superstar in school. One kindergarten Hmong girl answered shyly, "When teacher says my name right."

From the very first day of school, make it a solid intention to learn to pronounce each child's name correctly. If you are unfamiliar with the name, ask her to tell you how it is pronounced and make a mental (or written) note to yourself to remember. Avoid the practice of shortening names or giving Anglicized names to the students. Even if they have personally decided, as many do, to rename themselves in order to become more "accepted" in American society, be willing to ask them what their name preference really is and go by that. You will often find that they would prefer their given names if people would only pronounce them correctly. There are, however, many students who would rather shed their cultural roots at the door, having already been made to feel ashamed for their cultural identity. Perhaps another way for finding their true preference is to ask questions such as these: "Do you also have a Somali name? Can you tell me? What does it mean? I would love for the class to use your family name since we are your school family. Is that okay with you?"

TEACHER AS MODEL

It cannot be said too often that you, as the teacher, are the medium of your own message. No matter what you may be explicitly teaching in the curriculum, the hidden curriculum is always being communicated in the normal, everyday ways in which you live your life and interact with people both inside and outside of school. The children notice everything you do! The clothes you wear, the foods you eat, your tone of voice, the way you speak to them and to others (both verbally and through body language), and the friendships you establish are all noted by your students. The following are suggestions for capitalizing on this fact and furthering your CRT goals.

Sample Ways a Teacher Can Serve as Model

Wearing Diversity

Ellie, an exemplary third-grade teacher, literally wears her appreciation for diversity. She says, "I just love the different ways people dress, and I try to show appreciation for cultures in my own apparel. I have Navajo and Zuni bracelets from local powwows, hair clips from travels in Africa, a Russian shawl from a neighborhood second-hand store, a short kimono, called a haori, from a Japanese department store, a shirt from a friend in Nigeria, silver earrings from Indonesia, and a necklace from a local Cinco de Mayo celebration. My wardrobe brims with diversity! I love it when the kids touch these items and ask about them. They always notice, and that gives me a chance to share some information and enthusiasm about where and from whom I bought them or how I was gifted. It also stimulates my students to bring clothing and other cultural items to school and share what these things mean to them."

You, too, can demonstrate your love for diversity by wearing a scarf or a shirt, a tie, a pin or a hat that you bought during your travels or at a powwow, a cultural fair, or someone's church or temple bazaar in your students' local neighborhood. You needn't (and shouldn't) outfit yourself in anyone's full traditional regalia to make your point. Small

(Continued)

(Continued)

items are most appropriate and sufficient and usually noticeable to the children. They will probably ask you about what you are wearing, but if they don't, you can mention it. This is a good opportunity to converse and impart your interest in the many flavors of diversity of clothing and adornment styles to be found globally, nationally, and right in your own school community.

Food for Thought

As an additional note on this subject, please be aware that traditional clothes are not always the daily garb of young people in numerous cultures. Many children in our country and throughout the world wear jeans, T-shirts, and sneakers as normal, everyday attire, and traditional clothes only for ceremonies and celebrations. Others do wear traditional or combinations of traditional and modern western clothes. Be attentive to accurately reflecting the children of today in the pictures and books of your classroom. This is a good topic for discussion.

Upon first examination, this mode of "wearing diversity" may seem somewhat superficial in that it doesn't begin to address any culture in a comprehensive way. But that is not the point in this instance. You are creating a "culture-safe" classroom here. The intention is for you to establish yourself in your students' eyes as one who appreciates diversity in people and all things, and from such openers, you will find them feeling increasingly safe to offer their own cultural statements and contributions to your class community.

Eating Diversity

If you eat snacks or lunch with your students, include a diversity of foods in your lunchbox: sushi, tacos, gyros, spanakopita, fry bread, etc. Let them see that you are open to tasting and trying the infinite choices of cultural foods. In this way, you will find them bringing you all kinds of treats and family specialties, and you have opened one more door that allows your students to feel both pride in their own culture and appreciation of the cultures of others. Be sure to try them! And be enthusiastic. If health laws allow it, have parents bring snacks from their traditions, or you can be the one to bring multicultural snacks to share on a weekly basis. Discuss how different cultures enjoy different tastes and that the most tastes we can learn to appreciate, the more well-rounded and "cosmopolitan" we become (Appiah, 2007). (Include this word, *cosmopolitan*, meaning "a person who feels at home all over the world" and "one who feels at home *with people from* all over the world" in your class vocabulary of positive attributes.)

Diverse Relationships

When I was a young, novice teacher, I taught in a run-down city neighborhood in a school that served children living in the local public housing project. My dingy classroom with opaque windows was the only one in the school basement. In those days, Culturally Responsive Teaching was definitely not part of my school's value system or focus. I was easily saddened by the harsh life issues of poverty that many of my young pupils were facing, as well as the unwelcoming smoke-filled faculty room of colleagues who seemed to have no welcome or support for me, a young newcomer to the region. Most of my colleagues demonstrated little interest in the fertile cultural variety of our students, and their racial biases were blatant. But I found friendship and great support from the elder custodian, of an ethnicity other than my own, whose boiler room office was across the hall from my room. His kindness both to me and to my students was a welcome gift. I found I could count on him for all kinds of assistance and encouragement when I needed it. We shared many stories and jokes. His friendly pop-ins at my door, his hearty greetings to the kids in the hall, and his infectious laughter were lights in the darkness both for myself and for my pupils. He was my best friend in that school. I hope our friendship supported him too in that lonely role he played within the school hierarchy. I also realize now how valuable it was for my students to observe our friendship. This was an opportunity for them to witness respectful and friendly adult interactions across different roles and educational "status" and between differing ages, races, and genders within the school culture.

Be aware of how the children are perceiving your relationships with other people. Who are your friends among the staff? Do you greet the custodian or a parent with the same interest and respect that you greet a teaching colleague or the principal? Whose pictures do you have on your desk? Who do your bring into your class to share their knowledge and skills with your students? For your sake and for your students, learn to cultivate relationships across racial, ethnic, age, gender, sexual orientation, education, and economic differences. Your friendships speak louder than words.

Community Presence

Go out of your way to get to know the families and communities of your students. Make it a point to be seen, at least monthly, at the places they go after school or on weekends: Girls and Boys Club events,

(Continued)

(Continued)

street fairs, cultural celebrations, or sports events. Put yourself in situations where you are in the minority, such as a church, a synagogue, temple, or mosque that is not your own religious or ethnic comfort zone. (You will learn a great deal from this exercise, including the discomfort one can sometimes feel when one is in the minority. . . an anxiety many of your students may feel at school.) Frequent the family businesses in your school neighborhood. Bring the whole class to various events. If possible, allow your students to be your hosts. Willingly go to their homes if invited (Saifer, Edwards, Ellis, Ko, & Stuczynski, 2011). This will give you immeasurable ways to know your students and their families. Chat with parents and grandparents after school and invite them to share their knowledge and skills with the students when appropriate for the curriculum. (These can be ascertained by a questionnaire at the beginning of the school year or in subsequent

Food for Thought

If you, as an individual or as a faculty, do decide to conduct home visits, I suggest that you read the chapter "Creating Responsive Learning Through Home Visits," in Marjorie Ginsberg's book, *Transformative Professional Learning* (2011, pp. 55–80). This section will give you valuable information on the ways in which home visits can be beneficial exchanges for you, your students, and their families. Preparing well for the event is essential. Knowing what kinds of questions to ask and being able to collect and record important information about your student while being a good listener are important considerations. Having some advanced knowledge about the protocol of family interactions, such as what clothes are appropriate to wear, what social norms the family holds for greetings, and what are some of the family gender expectations, is most valuable. If you have not yet experienced a home visit, do not be discouraged by these considerations, but read and discuss this chapter with your colleagues. There is so much indispensable information and warm connection to be gained by learning about your students' cultural backgrounds and establishing a friendly rapport with their families. Although home visits will be time consuming at the year's beginning, you will find that your exposure to your students' lives will help you avoid the incalculable time expenditures resulting from cultural misunderstandings or conflicting expectations between you and your students or between school and home cultures. If you have the support of the school faculty and principal, this is all the better for your investment in home visits.

conversations.) As mentioned earlier, make attempts to learn at least a few words in their languages. Although a teacher's life is a busy one, and your own private time is essential for your well-being, your visibility in the children's communities will have a powerful and lasting effect on them and their families. It will also serve you immeasurably in your own growth toward deeper understanding and enjoyment of the flavors each child brings to the community of your classroom, as well as to the larger American culture.

SELF-REFLECTIVE TEACHING STYLE

Be mindful of how you interact with your students in the teaching and learning process. In particular, learn to be thoughtfully responsive, rather than automatic or reactive with your students. Become conscious of yourself as you are seen by them. Self-reflection, which generates self-awareness and self-renewal, is the only way to develop the essential knowledge and skills required to be a good culturally responsive teacher (Gay, 2003). Constantly ask self-reflective questions that help you to expand your abilities in this area, and establish ways of evaluating yourself. With this, as in all aspects of Culturally Responsive Teaching, you may want to arrange for reciprocal peer observations with colleagues, using tallies, checklists, and anecdotal reports. Although these subjects will be developed more fully in later chapters, here are a few reflective questions to ask yourself:

Self-Reflective Questions

Inclusive Eyes

Do I make certain that my eyes include all the children when I am talking to the group?

Praise and Feedback

Do I give the same amount of praise, feedback, constructive advice, and remediation to all the children?

Open-Ended Questions

Rather than always quizzing for right answers, am I interested in my students' different points of view, asking open-ended questions that will elicit their perspectives?

(Continued)

(Continued)

Promoting Response

Do I make certain to give everyone, including my English Learners, a chance to respond, not just the more vociferous and vocal ones?

Fair-Minded Classroom Management

Am I self-observant about who gets the most feedback for positive and negative behavior? What kind of behaviors in them does *my* behavior elicit or reinforce? Are my discipline interventions more instructive than punitive? Am I conscious of ways I may be favoring certain students over others?

Understanding Your Reactions

Do I have any negative reactions to certain students or their behaviors that could be more deeply understood? Do I have personal reactions to those who have different cultural styles from mine?

Awareness of Cultural Communication Styles

Am I becoming increasingly aware of different cultural styles in voice volume, needs for space or distance, showing affection, expressing passion, eye contact protocol, dealing with conflict, and responding to direct or nondirect questions?

Enthusiasm

Deidre, a second-grade colleague, was tired and often angry with her students. She was a troubled teacher who should have either been counseled or retired but was, instead, shunted to our low-income city school with youngsters of a variety of cultural backgrounds. She was not prepared for the culture shock of so many differences in learning and behavior styles. Deidre's tone of voice was harsh and critical. "Shut up!" was a phrase I often heard across the hall from my room, and my own students would sit up with startled attention. While Deidre had the competence and experience to teach second-grade skills with thoroughness and precision, her lack of emotional warmth and her irritability deeply sabotaged her students' ability to learn. Their lack of self-control, test scores, and general apathy reflected their unhappiness and agitation in that depressed environment.

Am I lighthearted, or do I often find myself complaining or criticizing? Do I use uplifting humor whenever possible? Do I love life and learning and seek to demonstrate my enthusiasm to the kids? If not, what are some changes I need to make to shift my tone for the sake of my students? (When a teacher's enthusiasm is missing, there are countless negative repercussions for the students.)

Sensitivity to Emotion

Am I constantly receptive to the spoken or unspoken messages from my students, knowing immediately when they are bored, uncomfortable, hurt, sad, angry, or frustrated?

Responsiveness

Am I responsive to these things? In other words, am I consciously changing or modulating my thinking patterns and beliefs, my expectations of myself, and my behaviors to enhance their learning experience in all ways possible?

As we have discussed earlier, a teacher's unconscious behaviors and reactions to students comprise much of the hidden curriculum and have a decisive effect upon the learner's success. The culturally responsive teacher strives to become continually aware of unconscious patterns through self-reflection (Ginsberg, 2011).

You will have many opportunities for self-observation, discussion, and evaluation in the chapters to come. But these questions above offer a good beginning. Honest self-inquiry is a necessary portal for deeper personal understanding of yourself and your relationships with your students, and it offers greater growth to you as a CRT professional.

If your students are resistant to you in any way, it is essential to bravely ask yourself how you might change to make them feel more comfortable with you and the environment of their school. As my husband, Gary Howard, always says to his workshop participants, "It is important that as culturally responsive teachers we regularly ask ourselves a courageous question: 'What might I be doing in my classroom that is getting in the way of my students' learning?' We ask this question not because we are bad teachers but because we are passionately concerned with our students' success." The culturally responsive teacher is not defensive or quick to judge or blame students or their families for their struggles, but rolls up his sleeves to find win/win solutions for all involved. Culturally responsive teachers are resilient and confident. If children have not been too badly traumatized by life, they are usually extremely forgiving and want very much to be in the good graces of their teacher.

The Red Ribbons of Culturally Responsive Teaching call you to see yourself as your students' greatest advocate and to be self-aware about how they are affected by you in every moment of the day. Remember, you are creating memories in your classroom for each child, and you are creating the nest for their success in the world. Intentionally incorporating *Personal Connections* with each student in the cycles of your days, consciously fashioning yourself as a culturally responsive *Teacher as Model*, and adopting a *Self-Reflective Teaching Style*, are simple, but profound ways to help you develop greater warmth, respectfulness, and graciousness with your diverse students and their families. We weave the Red Ribbons into our practice because we want to rally our students to enthusiastic learning with us and because we want life in our classroom to be rich and memorable for everyone.

RED RIBBONS

QUESTIONS TO PONDER AND DISCUSS

Utilize these questions for personal reflection or group discussion with colleagues.

- Do you believe that relationship is the foundation of good teaching and learning?
- Who was your favorite teacher? How would you describe your relationship with this teacher? In what ways did this teacher make you feel good and safe in the class environment?
- Make a list of his or her characteristics or behaviors that made you feel ready, willing, and excited to learn?
- What are the ways in which this teacher addressed the uniqueness of each student? Did he or she make them feel gifted or special? How?
- Now try to recall the worst teacher you ever had. What was lacking in this teacher's manner and approach to you and to your classmates?
- List his or her characteristics or behavior that got in the way of relationship and learning.
- How did this "worst teacher" deal or not deal with the many differences in his or her students?
- Are you a lifelong learner? What are your current interests and passions? What of these would you like to share with students?
- What does the focus of the Red Ribbons inspire in *you*, personally and professionally?
- List five of your qualities that already make you personally and culturally inviting as a teacher.
- What worries, concerns, or questions do you have about the Red Ribbons?

- In what way(s) can you improve upon your *Personal Connections* with students to enhance your CRT teaching strategies?
- List and discuss ways you can capitalize upon the concept of *Teacher as Model* to increase your set of CRT skills.
- Do you consider yourself to have the capacity for a *Self-Reflective Teaching Style*? In what ways do you see yourself in this light?
- Do you recognize the need for this ability to enhance your personal and professional development? Why?
- What creative ideas and suggestions do you have to enhance a teacher's ability to be personally and culturally inviting?

RED RIBBONS RESOURCES
PERSONAL CONNECTIONS

MANY WAYS TO SAY "HELLO" AND "GOOD-BYE"

- Mantra Lingua Hello Poster in 36 Languages
  http://usa.mantralingua.com/

- Educational Poster Chart: Goodbye in 28 Different Languages
  http://www.amazon.co.uk/Goodbye-28-Different-Languages-Educational/dp/B000QVYHMU

Orange Ribbons 3

*The Classroom Is Personally
and Culturally Inviting*

---

*How do you insure that your students have a positive sense of belonging
and are affirmed? This is critical when designing a culturally compatible
environment for students of any age.*

—Barbara Shade, Cynthia Kelley, and Mary Oberg
Creating Culturally Responsive Classrooms

Now that the students are warmly received by you at the doorway of learning, what else do they experience upon entering the world of the culturally responsive classroom? It is important to be intentional about making the classroom itself a conspicuously welcoming venue for your invitational CRT work. Most elementary teachers have very colorful, warm, and attractive classrooms already, as my years of teaching among creative colleagues have demonstrated to me. However, it is the purpose here to make your classroom even more invitational and conducive to learning for all.

As you proceed through this chapter, keep in mind two more of our Vertical Threads:

- **Context Is as Important as Content**
  and
- **Everything Can Be Seen From Multiple Perspectives**

Review these two important mindsets from the Vertical Threads chapter. As you consider the fundamental importance of context as a teaching tool, you can be increasingly aware of, and deliberate about, the culturally responsive ethos and values you want them to absorb in the atmosphere of your teaching space (Hammond, 2015). And the capacity for multiple perspectives is an important frame of mind for the children to develop in classrooms composed of many cultures and races. Indeed, it has become a vital life skill for living in a pluralistic society! Continue to keep yourself open to the kind of self-reflection that will unearth static beliefs and assumptions in these categories about yourself and about your students.

Following are a few suggestions, in the four categories of *Addressing the Five Senses*, *Inclusive Curriculum and Reading Materials*, *Universal Monthly Themes*, and *Circle Corner* to stimulate your own ingenuity as you brainstorm with your coworkers the innumerable ways to do this. These foci should not stand alone, but be woven into weekly and monthly topics into which the learning objectives for reading, language arts, math, science, social studies, health, music, and art are easily incorporated. You will find many books and materials listed in the Orange Ribbons Resources. All are easy to access, available through Amazon.com unless otherwise indicated. Although there are several resources listed for Grades 4 and 5, please note that materials for primary age children can be utilized for older students in many ways: stimulating discussion on certain topics, simplifying important information, providing the texts for readers' theater or dramatizations for younger children, and in supporting the English Language Learners (ELL) students or slower readers of the class.

ADDRESSING THE FIVE SENSES

Food for Thought

Before discussing the "Addressing the Five Senses" approach, I want to offer one point of clarification. In some ways, a focus on the sensory aspects of Orange Ribbons could appear to be what is known in the CRT field as a simplistic "contributions approach," where food and dances, music, stories, and art are added to the curriculum without deeper understanding of the meaning of these practices within the cultures and without actually changing the structure of the curriculum to be beneficial for all students (Banks & Banks, 2013). This would be true if our focus was limited to only the surface aspects of culture. However, the Orange Ribbons activities presented here are designed to prime the pump, whet the appetite, and stimulate your passion and your students' readiness for CRT. Other essential aspects of comprehensive CRT are addressed in the "ribbons" of the following chapters.

So let us focus on the senses, knowing that this is an important beginning. As your students gaze around the room, what meets their eyes? What reflects or stimulates them? There are hundreds of ways to make your classroom a culturally responsive visible experience. Inclusion of a multiplicity of ethnic images and materials is a most important goal for the culturally responsive teacher who wants to make sure that all students feel welcome and safe (Saifer, Edwards, Ellis, Ko, & Stuczynski, 2011). Make your walls and ceilings, your windows, floors, and doors a tribute to your students' differences and to the rich diversity of our nation and world.

Food for Thought

It is essential to remember that there is diversity even in classrooms that have one primary ethnic group or gender. In classrooms composed of mostly European American students, for instance, you can highlight Polish, Scandinavian, Greek, and other diversities and then move into discovering aspects of cultures not represented by your students. Create ways, through the senses, to introduce new and interesting cultural information. In same-culture, same-gender classes, you can begin with diverse interests, hobbies, likes, and dislikes and then progress into discussing and learning about diversities outside of your classroom setting. Regardless of who comes through your doors, teach your kids a little about a lot of people, religions, cultures, etc. by representing many groups in your class environment.

From the moment your students enter the classroom in the morning to the end of the day, what kinds of sounds touch their ears? And how can sound be utilized to feature diversity in culture? Sound is a most wonderful and enjoyable stimulant to learning and can be employed by the culturally responsive teacher in a multitude of ways. In the same manner, touch is a sense that is often overlooked as a teaching tool yet is a most important one for young people, and especially for students with strong kinesthetic inclinations. What opportunities do your students have for touch and movement in the daily curriculum? And how can these senses support your CRT goals? Taste and smell are a little harder than the other senses to address in the classroom, especially since so many children have allergies, but they are such significant aspects of all students' cultural backgrounds, we should do our best to include them, at least in stories and discussions.

Sample Activities for Addressing the Five Senses

Phyllis, an older, seasoned teacher, was having a hard time relating to the rapid increase in cultural diversity of children now populating her suburban school and classroom. I was asked to coach her and provide strategies for how to improve her relationships with her students. She admitted that she felt uncomfortable with change, with diversity and "all this newness," and nostalgic for the "way things used to be." I encouraged her to take photos of her students in the classroom and on the playground. Perhaps, if she could distract herself in this way, she could step back from her fears of "difference" and appreciate her students through the "new eyes" of her camera. The next time I visited her class, I was amazed. Phyllis had taken my advice to heart. The walls were covered with beautiful, enlarged photos of her diverse young learners in all kinds of activities. Their bright-eyed facial expressions told me they were having a good time at school. She said that this approach had not only given her deeper appreciation and affection for her students but had inspired in her a new creative passion for photography, which was spilling over to them as well. She had procured some school funds to buy five more cameras for the kids, who were now working in teams, to "catch" their classmates doing interesting things. Many of the compelling photos that I was observing were, in fact, taken by her students.

Students' Photos

You, too, can take photos of your students or have them take photos of each other. Enlarge these to decorate the walls. Make certain that all pictures—photos, calendars, charts, and other teaching visuals—on the walls, as well as those in all books chosen for the curriculum, reflect the racial identities of diverse people.

Posters

Use posters that reflect America's ethnicities from community events, jazz festivals, ethnic celebrations, cultural plays, etc.

Morning Mirror

If you are teaching primary students, (K–3), and truly want to "reflect" them and their racial and ethnic identities in your classroom, utilize a full-sized mirror on the wall. At the opening of each day, have one or two students (individually) come up to the mirror to say, "I am the only one like me. I'm the greatest me I see!" Then ask them to tell you and the other students all the things they like about themselves. (You can fill in a few characteristics you love about them, too.) Make sure their lists of attributes build over time. This is a wonderful ritual that develops self-esteem in your students and helps them all see how diverse are our talents and gifts. Of course, some of your students, as a function of personality and/or culture, may not be comfortable at first with so direct a focus on their individuality, so allow this to be a voluntary activity, especially in the beginning. But you will find most of your students warming to the practice as the year progresses.

My class of first graders loved the Morning Mirror ritual and would often describe themselves as chocolate, mocha, or vanilla ice cream, depending on their skin color. However, I was not given those options, probably due to my Scottish Irish heritage of pink cheeks. "Not you, Mrs. Howard," they told me. "You're strawberry!"

Food for Thought

Here I will make a brief statement about children's racial identity. Some teachers, particularly white teachers, are uncomfortable with any mention of skin color or race. Wanting to be respectful, they avoid the subject altogether, sometimes claiming that they don't "see color" in their students. As mentioned earlier, this is what has come to be known in CRT circles as "color blindness" and is actually a disservice to students, who feel that a teacher who is not observant of their color (and their ethnicity) doesn't really see them for who they are. From at least four years of age, children are acutely aware of differences in the color of hair, eyes, and skin, as well as many other distinguishing characteristics. Without the crippling attitudes of racism and prejudice from the society around them, children would take skin color difference in the same nonjudgmental stride as differences in hair color or body size. If skin color/tone is as comfortably recognized by you as any other aspect of your students' unique identities, then conversations and comments, such as in the story above, flow naturally and respectfully in the classroom. It was the children who introduced the routine of comparing themselves to ice cream—all delicious

(Continued)

(Continued)

flavors—and I merely allowed, and enjoyed, the natural evolution of the ritual. (Some students may be tainted, already, with racial attitudes from their families and social environments, however. The establishment of a stigma-free classroom is one of your first priorities—but not by denying your students' identities.) (See the Violet Ribbons chapter for *Dealing Directly With Prejudice*.)

Community Photos

Have your students take photos of members of the diverse community beyond the school's boundaries—perhaps with topics that arise from reading or writing lessons, such as Elders, Little Children, Mothers, Fathers, Pets, etc. Have these pictures enlarged as well to enhance your classroom walls.

Cultural Art Everywhere

Engage your students in learning about and participating in different kinds of cultural art (kites, fabric designs, lanterns, dream catchers, medicine wheels, mandalas, papier maché piñatas, calligraphy, sand painting, basketry. . . there are so many possibilities). When these projects revolve around cultural monthly themes, or social studies units, all the better. One of the favorite projects in my classroom was a huge dragon "mascot" stuffed with wads of paper, decorated with scales cut, pasted, and sprinkled with glitter by each child. This activity brightened the room and tied in with our universal dragon theme for the month. If possible, bring in community members to demonstrate these cultural arts. There are many books for art projects for children from specific cultures. For an exceptional collection of global projects for kids, I have found the best online resource to be Pinterest.

See ORANGE RIBBONS RESOURCES: Addressing the Five Senses: Cultural Art.

Be sure to do your research to make certain any project accurately reflects a culture (i.e., Coastal Indians did not live in teepees!) Also, be certain to make a distinction between traditional and modern practices (i.e., most Native Americans of today live in modern homes). Furthermore, although genuine, traditional materials may be unobtainable and paper will have to do for many projects, make certain your students have a chance to at least see the real things in pictures or touchable artifacts.

Authentic Artists

When contracting artists-in-residence programs or asking local artists to share their work with your students, be sure to choose people who are representative of the culture they portray.

Thematic Collections

Make your own personal collections of items from many cultures around universal themes depicted in unique ways by different cultures. These can be displayed in a special place in your classroom throughout the year. Varieties of painted eggs from many cultures is such a theme. Clowns, baskets, calendars, counting devices, looms, nesting or stacking items, pottery, dolls, card games, and fans are the kinds of collections I gathered over the years which supported my monthly themes. These item collections are always good stimulants for discussion, especially at Circle Time. Encourage your students to add to the displays from their own cultural backgrounds.

Talent Presentations

At the beginning of the school year, have each child present her talents (often cultural talents) in some way. Talents can include singing, dancing, problem-solving, organizing, reading—anything at all! Take photographs of each child's presentation to make a bulletin board and later a class book of these presentations.

Make a Class Quilt

Have each child create a fabric square that represents him visually. (This can be done with fabric crayons on paper and later ironed onto the fabric squares.) Encourage your students to include cultural elements from their families as well as personal interests and talents. Give them a good amount of time to decide what they want to draw to depict themselves. Sew these together as a quilt for a wall hanging—a poignant, visual tribute to the unified diversity of your class community. As you proceed with this project, discuss or read together about the varieties of quilts and quilt patterns made in the United States and in the world (Asian and Asian American, Hispanics from many countries and Hispanic Americans, Native American, African and African American, European, Hawaiian), including the reasons and uses for them. (African American slave women placed quilts on the fence to warn or signal safe escape messages to others; women from many cultures had to make their blankets from used clothing when supplies were scarce, creating beautiful art from the materials available to them.)

Cultural Dollhouses

If you are a preschool or kindergarten teacher, comb through your local second-hand stores to include clothes, cooking utensils, decor, and other items in your doll and housekeeping corners that reflect the diverse home lives of your students. You can also ask parents for these kinds of donations.

(Continued)

(Continued)

World Music

Develop, or make sure your librarian orders, a collection of ethnic music that can be played for a variety of purposes. For example, you can use different cultural music for relaxing, for thinking, for creating, for cleaning up. Music for dancing and moving the body. Welcoming music. Calming music. Uplifting music, etc. If your school's cultural collection is in the beginning stages, use district level resources or a public library.

See ORANGE RIBBONS RESOURCES: Addressing the Five Senses: Cultural Music, Games, and Dances.

Global Instruments

Collect an assortment of rhythm instruments from a variety of cultures with which the students can experiment and learn to play. Many can be handmade by the students themselves. Again, use district level resources, if available. Rhythm instruments can be utilized for start and stop signals, cleanup time alerts, and any number of moments you need to get their attention. Let the students take turns doing this for you. Instruments are always useful for accompanying various dances and songs.

Multicultural Songs

Open the day with songs from various cultures. Rounds are great fun. So are chants. Simple harmonies are easy to learn with repetitive chants.

World Dances

Teach folk and cultural dances from a variety of cultures or collaborate with the PE teacher to include these in the curriculum. Have the students teach *you* some steps to their ethnic dances, such as the currently popular styles of African American hip-hop dancing, Irish step-dancing, Appalachian clogging, Native American fancy dancing, Mexican American salsa, Hawaiian hula. Even if you feel you have no rhythm, or two left feet, be humbly willing to try the steps that won't put your back out! Your students will appreciate your ability to "let down" and "get down" from time to time. Develop culturally varied music and/or dance performances for a parents' tea or a PTA night. If you have students who are physically challenged, be sure to include them in supportive ways, such as bringing them into the middle of a circle dance with a rhythm instrument they have chosen. Ask other students to join them in this role.

Cultural Musicians or Dancers

Invite in cultural musicians or dancers or take the students on field trips to community performances.

Chanting and Counting

Use ethnic chanting rhythms or counting in different languages as alerts for activity changes or clean-up time.

Clapping and Body Slapping

Rhythmic clapping and body slapping games are good signals for attention and excellent strategies to energize the group when the students start to feel "droopy."

Nature's Diverse Sounds

The recorded sounds from a forest, the ocean, the desert, or a field of flowers and insects can be utilized to enjoy and engender discussion about the beauty and value of nature's diversity.

Universal Games

Some games, such as jacks, are universal. I've seen it played among desert Intjartnama children of Australia, island children of Bali, and kids in the mountains of Nepal. This is a good discussion topic: "How is this possible that children in cultures so very far away from each other would be playing the same games passed down from the time before kids had access to television or computers?" Learning how to play this game with various cultural props (jacks, stones, coins) is a nonpedantic lesson in universality. Tick-Tac-Toe is another game with a long multicultural history. Children played this game in Egypt over 3,000 years ago.

Varieties of Stories

Include cultural music and stories on CDs in the listening corner with earphones for independent work. Some literacy series come equipped with excerpted stories from around the globe. Try to introduce music and objects that relate to the stories.

> See ORANGE RIBBONS RESOURCES: Addressing the Five Senses: Cultural Touch and Tastes

Global Fabrics

Gather fabrics of a variety of textures and designs from various ethnicities to use as pillows or throws in the circle or reading corner, as backgrounds for bulletin boards, as tablecloths or jackets for the students' books, or as mantles to put unfinished class projects to bed for the night.

Varieties of Texture

Make your thematic collections touchable. Rough, smooth, silky, bumpy, soft, and hard textures are a part of the artistic creations of all cultures and interesting to the touch.

(Continued)

(Continued)

World Grains

Have a World Grains Day (or month) and feature tortillas, rice cakes, wheat bread, fry bread, cornbread, pita, nan, etc. (Be certain to ascertain whether or not any of your students have celiac or other grain allergies and provide choices appropriate for those with dietary restrictions.) The grains can be bought, cooked at school, or made by one of the parents (preferably through demonstration), or the students can bring tasting samples to class. Focus on the aromas and tastes of these different creations from grain. All kinds of reading and writing projects can flow from such a focus. Many math objectives can be addressed as well, creating questions such as: "How do we divide all this *tteok* (Korean rice cakes) evenly among us?" (*Tteok* is about sharing. It is never meant to be eaten alone.) Or: "If we need to double this recipe for cornbread, how much of each ingredient do we need?"

Brain research tells us that music, movement, art, and discussion are the very stimuli that help us best to think (Tate, 2010). What better way to engage our full participation in CRT than to begin with multicultural sensory input? These Addressing the Five Senses activities are important beginning steps that will, throughout this and the next *Bright Ribbons* chapters, invite all your students into greater academic success. Furthermore, they will pave the way for the deeper, more comprehensive territory of democratic citizenship discussed in further chapters—citizenship that requires the capacity for critical thinking, the ability to ask courageous questions about social realities, and the will to offer creative solutions to the healing of inequity and injustice.

INCLUSIVE CURRICULUM AND READING MATERIALS

It is of utmost importance that the literature in your classroom accurately and authentically represents your students. Many studies have concluded that books that represent children of color are positively correlated with these students' motivation, engagement, and proficiency in reading. Yet, in spite of this and the increasing diversity in our schools, such books, as well as authors of color, are still not featured enough in many school libraries and classrooms (Hughes-Hassell, Barkley, & Hoehler, 2009). Comb through your class library and textbook collection to make certain that all materials contribute to the community of respect and inclusivity that you are cultivating in your classroom environment (Banks, 2008).

Create a checklist for yourself and with your school librarian and colleagues to analyze the culturally responsive quality of the materials, perhaps using the list of questions below. If you find books and textbooks to be lacking in inclusion, accurate information, and/or respect for all people, collaborate with your principal and fellow teachers to upgrade your school materials and resources.

The following list of questions will help guide your review of books and other materials.

Questions for Resource Evaluation

- Do the books present a wide range of the diversities of culture and ethnicity of American life?
- Are positive and authentic images of diverse families and communities portrayed in both the stories and the illustrations?
- Are authors of color well represented? (They should be, for there are many.)
- Do the materials teach students about the hardships and challenges, as well as the many contributions of various ethnic groups to our history?
- Do they honor the struggles and contributions of women in the evolving society?
- Do they offer positive and respectful images of gay, lesbian, and transgendered people?
- Do the materials, and the conversations they stimulate, help students think critically about the negative as well as the positive aspects of American society and history? (And can *you* accept the idea that to love one's country does not require denial of its harsh realities?)
- Do they engender a sense of fairness and a stance of responsibility toward upholding the rights of all people?

When you do come across previously undetected pictures, themes, or statements in your materials that are not respectful, true, comprehensive, or inclusive, feel free to discuss the matter with your students: "Why does this Social Studies book talk so much about wars?" "Why don't we learn about the peoples' lives affected by these events?" "What about the families?" "Where are the children?" "Did you notice that there are no women in this story?" "Why is that?" "How many different cultures and races of people did you notice in this book?" Elementary students have a strong, natural sense of justice and fairness that comes out in these discussions. Including them in the review of omissions and distortions in the classroom materials will teach them much about critical thinking and will reinforce the tone of kindness and respect that you are creating together in the environment.

UNIVERSAL MONTHLY THEMES

Everything you create in the setting of the classroom can reflect your intention to value our differences *as well as* our commonalities as human beings. In how many ways can you honor the beauty of differences and the differences of beauty? One suggestion is to use a universal subject as your monthly focal point. Rather than focusing on the same clichéd seasonal themes year after year, branch out. There are many possible topics. Ask your librarian for help in collecting books to augment them. Utilize search engines to find more information for yourself and for your students. There's much to learn at our fingertips. Following are several monthly themes I have employed in my classroom:

Sample Universal Monthly Themes

September: Dragons

All cultures that I am familiar with have some form of dragon or giant serpent in their ancient stories and iconography. A West African/Haitian rainbow serpent, Damballah Wedo, rules the skies with his wife, Ayida Wedo, the rainbow goddess. Australian Aboriginal people, too, honor the Rainbow Serpent (Gooriala, in the Lardil language), who created the world. One of the dragon's names in China is Shen, a revered designer of mirages who always carries a pearl of wisdom in his mouth. Quetzacoatl, the feathered serpent of knowledge and wisdom, arises from Mayan traditions. The Red Dragon of Wales, Y Ddraig Goch, is the symbol on the Welsh flag, supposedly carried by King Arthur into battle. Some cultures perceive dragons as scary and deadly, some revere them as benevolent and wise. I have found that children everywhere find dragons fascinating and awe-inspiring. I'm sure you have noticed that dragon stories abound in the children's and young adults' literature and movies of today. There is something about a dragon that stirs students' imaginations, and this can be capitalized upon in your curriculum. I discovered "dragon-ology" to be *the* most enticing theme of the year, and I wove it into my lesson plans for the month of September, a month for getting to know my students and making them feel welcome and enthused about learning in my classroom.

> See ORANGE RIBBONS RESOURCES: Universal Monthly Themes: September: Dragons.

October: Clowns and Tricksters

Eight-year-old Natalia was not allowed to participate in school Halloween festivities because of her family's religious beliefs. Not wanting to exclude her or discomfort her family, yet also not wanting to deprive the other children of the excitement they felt on this holiday, her teacher, Kevin, decided to insert a Clowns theme into the October calendar. Rather than celebrating Halloween, he called the month's culminating event Clown Day, which allowed his students to still dress up, albeit as clowns of the world, in a way that would include Natalia and serve the curriculum as well.

I love laughing, as do children. That's why I adopted Kevin's idea and enjoyed introducing clowns and tricksters into my seasonal themes. Clowns and tricksters are a universal phenomenon . . . every culture has them . . . and they are most contagious for learning. They are Raven among the native coastal people of North America, Bre'er Rabbit of the American South, Coyote in the American Southwest, Kama Puaa the giant pig in Hawaii, Anansi the spider in Ghana, the Sly Fox of all continents, the farmer Trang Quynh of Vietnam, and two potbellied characters in the shadow puppetry of Bali. Sometimes these trickster types reflect the challenges between the poor and the upper class. Clowns and tricksters can be insatiably hungry and constantly trying to trick others into getting their needs met. There are times they steal and cheat and lie and mirror very undesirable human tendencies. Sometimes they are more heroic and admirable. But they are always wily and ingenious. Young and old enjoy the moment when the trickster wins a deserved reward through cleverness or when the clown's chicanery backfires and the trickster becomes the victim. Allow your students to bring in examples of the clowns and tricksters in their cultural caches as you familiarize them with the tales you have discovered. You will have many opportunities for delightful conversations as you assign clown-illustrated math problems and tackle language or reading assignments with a trickster puppet in the mix. Be sure to discuss with your students the common love for laughter that we share as human beings.

See ORANGE RIBBONS RESOURCES: Universal Monthly Themes: October: Clowns and Tricksters.

Food for Thought

Regarding the Clown Day story above, because of the complexities and varieties of our religious belief systems, such a strategy may not work for all families, but try to be as creatively inclusive as you can.

(Continued)

(Continued)

November: Ways to Say "Thank You"

Because the U.S. Thanksgiving falls in November, it is a good month to feature the myriad of ways that gratitude is expressed throughout the many cultures and ethnicities of our country and world. You set the stage by learning about and teaching a variety of gestures, gift items, words, and rituals that are used to show appreciation to others or to honor the gifts of creation. The goddess of the harvest of corn and grain was honored in ancient Greece and Rome with great celebrations, feasting, and games. Our "cornucopia," the horn-shaped basket filled with fruits and flowers, dates back to those cultures. The festival "Chung Ch'ui" was celebrated in China to commemorate the harvest moon, where families feasted on round yellow cakes called "moon cakes." Fill a cornucopia with little cakes and/or fruits from a variety of cultures. Have your students add small scroll notes, tied with ribbons, about things they are thankful for. Letters of thanks to a variety of people in your school, your community, or the students' families would be a good language arts project.

> See ORANGE RIBBONS RESOURCES: Universal Monthly Themes: November: Ways to Say "Thank You."

Food for Thought

For November, I offer one caveat that a culturally responsive teacher needs to acknowledge. In our focus on Thanksgiving, it is important to recognize that not all Americans share in the gratitude story of the Mayflower Pilgrims. My friendships with Native Americans and teaching on an Indian reservation made me sensitive to this fact. One way to begin to address this is to focus on the Indians' knowledge of farming that saved the pilgrims from starvation and to discuss the basic thanks European settlers of Plymouth Colony owed to the native Wampanoag people for their survival. Of course, age appropriateness is required for discussing the severe realities of history. But it is first important for *you* to be knowledgeable about the facts beyond the myths and to introduce them wisely in due course. In the normal school curriculum, it is not generally known that within one generation, any blessings of that first Thanksgiving were not felt between the Wampanoag people and the pilgrims. Students can learn that when the settlers started aggressively encroaching on Native American land and the Indian fur trade dried up due to colonial competition, the Pequot War (also known as King Phillip's War) ensued. It was a bloody conflict that lasted three years and devastated the Wampanoag people and neighboring tribes. For your own information, you might want to read "The REAL Story of Thanksgiving" by Susan Bates, Native American newspaper columnist and children's book author. You can also watch her YouTube presentation: "The Truth About Thanksgiving" (Bates, n.d.).

December: Festivals of Light

With strong emphasis on the fact that not all cultures celebrate the coming of the light in the month of December (and, furthermore, it is summer in the southern hemisphere, when sunlight is at its zenith), I still utilize this month to make comparisons between several cultural holidays, since December in schools is often fraught with conflict about whether or not Christmas should be acknowledged and/or celebrated. My answer to the dilemma is not to censor Christian students' enthusiasm for the season, but to celebrate many festivals of light throughout the world, including the traditions of my students who are Jewish, Muslim, non-Christian Native American, Hindu, Buddhist, non-Christian African American, or nonreligious as well. The symbolism of "light" for us as humans is quite universal. It has always been used to honor rebirth and renewal and to represent the triumph over evil. *That* is something we can all celebrate! Children of Thailand observe Loi Krathong in November, making banana leaf boats to carry lighted candles, flowers, and coins down local rivers. The African American celebration of Kwanza honors African harvest traditions, lighting a candle each night for a week in December. The Festival of Northern Lights is celebrated in Ontario, Canada. Hanukkah, the Jewish Festival of Lights, is also celebrated by lighting a candle each night to remember the miracle of the sacred lamp oil in the temple lasting eight days, when it was only enough for one. The Scots, remembering Gaelic and Viking traditions, parade by torchlight in late December swinging burning fireballs.

There is so much light in the world and so many ways to celebrate it! Imagine your classroom glowing with tiny electric lights, battery operated tea lights, myriads of lanterns, and pictures of light in numerous traditions. Bring more light into your students' eyes by honoring the light in their family traditions and those of others.

See ORANGE RIBBONS RESOURCES: Universal Monthly Themes: December: Festivals of Light.

Food for Thought

If you are unsure of the legality of celebrating religious holidays in school, you may access "The Twelve Rules of Christmas" compiled by attorneys of the Rutherford Institute, which will apply to non-Christian religious festivals as well. Basically, public schools may teach about a religious holiday, "so long as it is taught objectively for secular purposes, such as historical or cultural importance, and not for the purpose of promoting [any religion]" (Rutherford Institute, 2015).

(Continued)

(Continued)

January: How to Celebrate a New Year

There are so many kinds of rituals and rites for New Year throughout the world! This month of our American New Year can be a wonderful introduction to expand your students' knowledge of the many ways humanity celebrates the passing of one year and the coming of the next. Of course, in this as in other date-related subjects, it must be emphasized that the calendars and days differ for these international celebrations. Make the students aware, too, that many traditional calendars are not based on a 12-month year. A monthly theme centering on the New Year presents a literal, as well as figurative, buffet of creative possibilities. New Year's food includes fritters (Dutch), bannocks (Irish), 12 grapes (Spanish), rice (Indian and Pakistani), apples dipped in honey (Jewish), and black-eyed peas and pork (southern United States). Some people paint their doors red for the New Year. Others dance in bear costumes. Gifts are given, and new leaves are turned over. Some folks celebrate with fireworks and the noise of church bells, drums, and guns. Others observe the day with quietude and prayer. But everyone celebrates the New Year in some way. This is a marvelous research topic for students. Have the class collaborate in making a multicultural class celebration for welcoming in the New Year in January.

But also draw your students' attention to when the Chinese New Year rolls around in late January or February, according to the Chinese calendar, and when the Jewish calendar celebrates its new year in Autumn. Make note with your students of other cultures' New Year's commemorations, too: "Today *Muharram*, the Islamic New Year, begins." "Today is *Songkran*, the Buddhist New Year festival in Thailand." To support you in this and other cultural lessons, it would be good, at the beginning of the school year, to avail yourself of a variety of cultural calendars, especially those of your students' cultures, putting reminders on your school calendar.

See ORANGE RIBBONS RESOURCES: Universal Monthly Themes: January: How to Celebrate a New Year.

February: Hundreds of Ways to Say "I Love You"

Love is an extensive subject, expressed in a myriad of ways in our vastly diverse world. Expand beyond the typical Hallmark Valentine's cards and posters into learning a multitude of gestures, gifts, and practices that people utilize to express love in a variety of cultures. Learn with your students the phrase, "I love you," in different languages. Ask your students to share special words or customs used in their families to express love. Organize a language arts unit around cultural varieties of poetry, the language of feeling that is an ancient form of communication and a universal way to convey love.

Explore with your students, through discussion or writing, just what aspects of this subject we are meaning to convey when we talk about love. "Are we discussing our love for our parents, or theirs for us?" "Are we examining our love for our friends, for our pets, for our sweethearts, for nature, or for a certain TV show?" "What are different words for different kinds of love?"

Your students will be interested in the fact that some cultures express love more through actions than words. Have older students discuss a quote from a person in Taiwan: "You Westerners use the word 'love' like chocolate sauce on ice cream. It's not necessary; the ice cream's already sweet enough." They can learn, too, that certain gestures of love in one culture may be too intimate to express publicly between people of another.

Focusing on the love of friendship is an age-appropriate subject for your students. You can acknowledge the fact that many of us have a special friend in elementary school. It is also good to emphasize that there is a certain kind of love the Greeks called "*agape*" which means love, respect, kindness, and consideration for all people, and even though we may have a very special friend or two, we practice *agape* in our class for each one of our classmates.

This month is also a good time to talk about ways people do *not* practice *agape* and continue to address the year-long subject of bullying, cliques, exclusivity, and animosity, as well as national and international strife and war. More will be discussed on this subject in the Violet Ribbons chapter, but the February season of love is a good time to emphasize *agape* and to be aware of how its antithesis can show up. Love is a wonderful topic for discussion for all ages and can increase your students' understanding about multiple perspectives, teaching them to be more loving toward each other, and to share their own unique family practices without fear of being judged.

> See ORANGE RIBBONS RESOURCES: Universal Monthly Themes: February: Hundreds of Ways to Say "I Love You."

March: Fairies and Invisible People

Go beyond featuring only leprechauns and shamrocks on your calendars and bulletin boards for March. Emphasize stories about fairies and invisible, or barely visible, people from all over the world. There are many examples: the Menehune of Hawaii, the Kobito of Japan, the Duendes of Argentina. Drums, rattles, and songs of the Yunwitsandsdi, the little music lovers of Cherokee legends, can sometimes be heard deep in the woods or in the mountains of northern Georgia and the Carolinas. Some "fairies" are large, such as the tall, thin Quinkins of Australia who are represented in cave paintings by Aboriginal people. Display fairies on the walls, hide

(Continued)

(Continued)

them in the desks, and weave them into the given lessons in all subjects. Invite your students to tell stories they might know of fairy-like creatures.

See ORANGE RIBBONS RESOURCES: Universal Monthly Themes: March: Fairies and Invisible People.

Access some readers' theater fairy tale scripts or create your own to perform for other classes. And have open-ended discussions, without expecting right or wrong answers, about why people around the world might think fairies and other barely visible people exist.

April: Eggs and Baskets

The egg on the Jewish seder plate for Passover and the Easter egg hunt that many Christian children enjoy are traditions that arrived in America on the winds of a long history of appreciation for the egg. In Western culture, the original sources of egg celebration were ancient pre-Jewish, pre-Christian rites of Earth-honoring cultures that revered the sacredness of the natural world, the egg being the symbol of life itself. From India to Polynesia, from countries of the Middle East to the west coast of South America, from the Baltic to Balkan nations, and from Central America to eastern Africa, ancient stories tell of the whole universe created out of an egg.

Decorating eggs has been practiced throughout the world for centuries. With golden eggs, red eggs, painted eggs, wooden, papier maché and enameled eggs, emu, ostrich, goose, chicken, and duck eggs, cultures on all continents have honored the egg for the new life it brings. Some traditions, such as the mounds of gilded eggs painted for the Tsar of Russia, were exceptionally lavish. Throughout the world, eggs are eaten, broken, smashed, painted, gilded, and dyed as representative of the miracle of life.

Baskets, too, are universal items, symbolizing the blessings of life and continual abundance. Swamp grass, sweet grass, cedar bark, pine needles, hickory bark, oak bark, palm leaves, or small vines have been utilized by cultures everywhere, from time immemorial, to weave the containers for collecting food, carrying water, gathering seeds, and holding babies. Baskets are such a universal item; there are certain to be cultural basket weavers in your area. Bring them in to demonstrate this ancient skill to your students.

Incorporate this month's theme into your science objectives, such as a study of birds and nests or learning about the seeds and eggs from which

See ORANGE RIBBONS RESOURCES: Universal Monthly Themes: April: Eggs and Baskets.

all living things come. The use of nature's bounty to support our common human survival needs can be woven into your social studies lessons. This month's theme could accommodate many aspects of your daily lesson plans.

May: Flowers

It was an unusually quiet moment in my classroom when all the students were in groups, with heads down, poring over and drawing the parts of the flowers that I had placed on each table. It was one of those memorable instances in my life as a teacher, where, not needing to inter-act with them for a few minutes, I was able to stand back and observe them in all their unique and precious aspects. In their varieties of color, size, shape, and personality, I saw all of my students as absolutely beau-tiful! In that one luscious moment, I felt there was nothing more exquisite in all the world than a garden of second graders.

As an elementary teacher and a gardener, I suppose it is natural for me to compare the collection of delightfully distinctive students to a flower gar-den, where appreciating the diversity of beauty in either setting can take your breath away. I invite you into this monthly theme to remind yourself, after a long year of teaching, just how priceless is each unique child in your class, and, in spite of the trials and challenges of your shared time with them, how lucky we are to have had these children in our lives for a year. Utilize May to center on flowers: flowers in the neighborhood flower shop, in our mothers' window boxes, in the local conservatory; flowers on trees, on fire escapes, and in the crevices of the sidewalks.

Make May baskets for elderly people in the community rest home. Because they are big seeds that grow fast, plant nasturtiums in pots on the windowsill. Bring in Science: "What kinds of flowers grow in differ-ent climates?" "What are the different stages of a flower's life?" "What are the parts of the flower?" "What do they need to flourish?" Health: "What do we, like flowers, need to flourish?" Social Studies: Read about the life of George Washington Carver, who rose from slavery to become a brilliant botanist. Art: There are many, many cultural art projects that will enhance your Flow-ers theme for May.

During Circle Time, pass around a multihued bouquet of flowers to engender a discussion about how all types of flowers have their own beauty and purpose . . . and how amazing they look all together! Flowers, because they are so beautifully diverse, are a perfect culminating monthly theme for a culturally responsive year in your classroom.

> See ORANGE RIBBONS RESOURCES: Universal Monthly Themes: May: Flowers.

CIRCLE CORNER

The Circle Corner has always been the heart of learning in my classroom, and I recommend it highly. Sitting in circles is a practice of cultures on all continents. In circles around the fire, in homes, kivas, longhouses, or groves, while talking, singing, dancing, or sitting in silence, the circle has been utilized for centuries in many cultures as a natural cohesive arrange-ment, building a sense of community, respect, and belonging within a society.

The experience of sitting in a circle is far different than sitting in rows. In a circle, we can all look into each other's eyes. No one stands above the others, and thus, although the teacher always has authority in the lives of the students, everyone in the circle is *felt* to have equal value and place in the community, especially when the Circle Time guidelines are followed. (This will be discussed more fully in the Yellow Ribbons chapter.) Sitting in a circle engenders a greater sense of personal responsibility for sharing one's own point of view and for upholding the healthy functioning of the group.

Your Circle Corner can be used as a space for reading to oneself or a partner and an area to engage in direct teaching, discussion, or small group instructions. But it should be large enough to comfortably hold all the students during your Morning Circle and Closing Circle times of the day. A large class may have to sit more in a bunch than a circle. Ideally, you can define the Circle Corner space with low bookshelves, a large circular rug, big pillows for the students to sit on, and a rocking chair for you. Do what you can to make it cozy.

The Circle should have something in its center, to provide focus and a sense of the significance of Circle Time. Fabrics from a variety of cultures are good centers. I have used my green Russian shawl or a piece of indigo fabric from Morocco and set my shell or stone collections upon them. Some teachers use "flowers, feathers, or a selection of talking pieces . . . " (Clifford, n.d.). Such "center pieces" can be stored in a special place. Students can take turns retrieving and arranging these for the day's Circle Times.

We have already mentioned a few discussions that can take place in this circular space, and more will be said about the use of Circle Time in the Yellow Ribbons chapter, but I include the Circle Corner space in this Orange Ribbons chapter simply to point out that there is nothing in the sensate structure of a classroom that is more invitational and more community-building than the Circle Corner.

This is the place where a sense of belonging is experienced viscerally and emotionally by students and teacher alike. My fourth and fifth graders appreciated it as much as my kindergartners and primary pupils. Within the circle individual identity is honored, cooperation is engendered, and a sense of group spirit is fostered. There is something about the inclusive roundness of the space and the marking of the days' cycles within it that sets the stage for the tone and trust that are exceptionally conducive to culturally responsive learning throughout the rest of the day.

Hopefully, these few suggestions will serve as catalysts for a lifetime of interest in creating the sensory and thematic classroom environment for Culturally Responsive Teaching to thrive. You are the weaver, after all, of your own artistic pedagogy. *Addressing the Five Senses*, incorporating *Inclusive Curriculum and Reading Materials*, utilizing *Universal Monthly Themes*, and establishing a *Circle Corner* are some of the ways to begin making your classroom a bright Orange Ribbon for your growing competence in CRT.

ORANGE RIBBONS

QUESTIONS TO PONDER AND DISCUSS

Utilize these questions for personal reflection or group discussion with colleagues.

- What are your current beliefs about the idea that Context Is as Important as Content? How do you see these beliefs changing for you?
- How does the Vertical Thread of Context Is as Important as Content relate to the Orange Ribbons?
- Is the concept of Multiple Perspectives new to you? What are your current beliefs about the concept that Everything Can Be Seen From Multiple Perspectives?
- In what ways do you see the Orange Ribbons weaving around the Vertical Thread of Everything Can Be Seen From Multiple Perspectives?
- What messages do you think children of color receive if they don't see themselves or their cultures reflected in the images, resources, and sensory materials of the learning space?
- What do you imagine are the benefits for children of color in a classroom that reflects their individual and cultural distinctiveness? In what ways would it enhance their learning?
- What are the benefits for white children in a classroom that reflect more ethnic diversity in its atmosphere than the traditional classroom?
- Are you willing to make a commitment to *Addressing the Five Senses* as a portal for Culturally Responsive Teaching?
- Make a list of at least 10 ways you would like to begin incorporating an *Addressing the Five Senses* approach.

(Continued)

(Continued)

- Seeing through the lens of Culturally Responsive Teaching, how would you conduct a resource upgrade to fairly reflect and do justice to all your students?
- In what ways would adopting *Universal Monthly Themes* be a useful and interesting approach to enhance your curriculum?
- List some ideas for similar themes that you might want to introduce? What topics arise from your normal grade-level curriculum?
- Have you established a *Circle Corner* or worked in a classroom that has one? List the ways you think this space benefits, or will benefit, your students? (More ideas will come in the Yellow Ribbons chapter.)
- What barriers or challenges (if any) do you have that would hinder you going forward in making your classroom a venue for Culturally Responsive Teaching?

ORANGE RIBBONS RESOURCES

(All resources available from Amazon.com
unless otherwise indicated.)

ADDRESSING THE FIVE SENSES

CULTURAL ART

- **Books**
  - *Art From Many Hands: Multicultural Art Projects*
    by Jo Miles Schuman, (2003) Davis
  - *Kids Around the World Create!: The Best Crafts and Activities From Many Lands*
    by Arlette N. Braman, (1999) John Wiley & Sons
  - (adult) *Hidden in Plain View: A Secret Story of Quilts and the Underground Railroad*
    by Jacqueline L. Tobin & Raymond G. Dobard, (2000) Anchor
  - *The Keeping Quilt*
    by Patricia Polacco, (2001) Simon & Schuster
  - *Luca's Quilt*
    by Georgia Guback, (1994) Greenwillow
  - *Most Loved in All the World*
    by Tonya Hegamin & Cozby Cabrera (illus., (2008) HMH
  - *Nonie's Magic Quilt*
    by Anita Vachharajani, (2014) DC Books
  - *The Quiltmaker's Gift*
    by Jeff Brumbea & Gail deMarcken, (2001) Orchard
- **Website**
  - Pinterest www.pinterest.com
    *Sign for a Pinterest account
    *Search by Culture (i.e., African Art for Kids; Japanese Art for Kids; Mexican Art for Kids, etc.)

CULTURAL MUSIC, GAMES, AND DANCES

- **CDs**
  - "A Child's World of Lullabies—Multicultural Songs for Quiet Times"
    by Hap Palmer, www.happalmer.com

- o "Hunk-Ta-Bunk-Ta Chants"
  by Katherine Dines
  Several sources—Google Katherine Dines

- o "Nature Sound"
  www.naturesound.org

- o "Nature Sounds Relaxation"
  World Music and Travel
  www.partnersinrhyme.com

- o Any of many Putumayo Kids CDs such as:
  "World Playground"
  "Dreamland"

- **CDs, Videos, and Books**
  - o *Teaching Movement and Dance*
    by Phyllis Weikart
    Several sources—Google Phyllis Weikart

- **Rhythm Instruments (authentic)**
  - o *from Lark in the Morning*
    Retail catalogue (877) 964-5569
    www.larkinthemorning.com

- **Rhythm Instruments (less expensive, not authentic):**
  - o Google: Rhythm Instruments for Kids

- **Books**
  - o *Acker Backa Boo!: Games to Say and Play From Around the World*
    by Opal Dunn & Susan Winter, (2006) Francis Lincoln

  - o *Can You Count Ten Toes?: Count to 10 in 10 Different Languages*
    by Lezlie Evans & Denis Roche, (2004) HMH

  - o *Dance Down the Rain, Sing Up the Corn: American Indian Chants and Games for Children*
    by Millie Burnett, (1975) R & E Research

  - o *Jingle Dancer*
    by Cynthia Leitich Smith, Ying-Hwa Hu, & Cornelius Van Wright (illus.), (2000) HarperCollins

- **Book and Tape**
  - o *Let Your Voice Be Heard! Songs From Ghana and Zimbabwe*
    by Abraham K. Adzenyah, Judith Cook Tucker, & Dumisani Maraire, (1997) World Music/Plank Road

- **Books**
  - *Step It Down: Games, Plays, Songs and Stories From the Afro-American Heritage*
    by Bessie Jones & Bess Lomax-Hawes, (1987) University of Georgia

  - *Play With Us: 100 Games From Around the World*
    by Oriol Ripoll, (2005) Chicago Review

- **Websites**
  - Jacks
    www.mastersgames.com/rules/jacks-rules.htm

  - Tic-Tac-Toe
    www.lucylearns.com/history-of-tic-tac-toe.html

Cultural Touch and Tastes

- **Books**
  - *Apple Pie Fourth of July*
    by Janet S. Wong & Margaret Chodos-Irvine (illus.), (2006) HMH

  - *Auntie Yang's Great Soybean Picnic*
    by Ginnie Lo & Beth Lo, (2012) Lee & Lo

  - *The Butter Man*
    by Elizabeth Alalou, Ali Alalou, & Julie Klear Essakalli (illus.),
    (2008) Charlesbridge

  - *Chicken Sunday*
    by Patricia Polacco, (1998) Puffin

  - *Cora Cooks Pancit*
    by Dorina K. Lazo Gilmore & Kristi Valiant (illus.), (2009) Shen's
    Books

  - *Dim Sum for Everyone!*
    by Grace Lin, (2014) Random House

  - *Dumpling Soup*
    by Jama Kin Rattigan & Lillian Hsu (illus.), (1998) Little Brown

  - *Everybody Cooks Rice*
    by Nora Dooley & Peter Thornton (illus.), (1992) Lerner/Carolrhoda

  - *Green Is a Chile Pepper*
    by Roseanne Greenfield Thong & John Parra (illus.), (2014)
    Chronicle

- ○ *Hiromi's Hands*
  by Lynne Brasch, (2007) Lee & Low

- ○ *Hot, Hot Roti for Dada-Ji*
  by F. Zia & Ken Min, (2011) Lee & Low

- ○ *I Have an Olive Tree (Greek)*
  by Eve Bunting & Karen Barbour (illus.),
  (1999) HarperCollins

- ○ *The International Cookbook for Kids*
  by Matthew Locricchio, (2012) Amazon

- ○ *Kids Around the World Cook: The Best Foods and Recipes From Many Lands*
  by Arlette N. Braman, (2000) John Wiley & Sons

- ○ *The Kids' Multicultural Cookbook: Food and Fun Around the World*
  by Deanna F. Cook & Michael Kline (illus.), (1995) Williamson

- ○ *Peach Heaven*
  by Yangsook Choi, (n.d.) Farrar, Strauss, & Giroux

- ○ *The Return of the Buffaloes: A Plains Indian Story About Famine and the Renewal of the Earth*
  by Paul Goble, (2002) National Geographic

- ○ *Round Is a Tortilla*
  by Roseanne Greenfield Thong & John Parra (illus.), (2013) Chronicle

- ○ *Too Many Tamales*
  by Gary Soto, (1996) Putnam & Grosset

UNIVERSAL MONTHLY THEMES

SEPTEMBER: DRAGONS

- **Books**
  - ○ *Chinese Cinderella and the Secret Dragon Society*
    by Adeline Yen Mah, (2004) HarperCollins

  - ○ "Constantes and the Dragon" in book: *Multicultural Fables and Fairy Tales*
    by Tara McCarthy, (1999) Scholastic

  - ○ *The Dragons Are Coming!*
    by Lotus Linton Howard & Dalton Webb (illus.), (2015) Amazon Kindle

- *Flying the Dragon*
  by Natalie Dias Lorenzi, (2012) Charlesbridge

- *Imagine a Dragon*
  by Laurence Pringle & Eujin Ki Neilan, (2008) Boyds Mills

- *Neem the Half Boy*
  by Idries Shah, Midori Mori (illus.), & Robert Revels (illus.),
  (2007) Hoopoe Books

- *The Rainbow Serpent*
  by Dick Roughsey & Percy Trezise, (1979) Angus & Robertson

- *Where the Mountain Meets the Moon*
  by Grace Lin, (2011) Little, Brown

- "Why the Red Dragon Is the Emblem of Wales" in book: *The
  Welsh Fairy Book*
  by W. Jenkyn Thomas, (2001) Dover

OCTOBER: CLOWNS and TRICKSTERS

- **Books**
  - *American Indian Trickster*
    by Richard Erdoes & Alfonso Ortiz (ed.), (1999) Penguin

  - *Jabuti the Tortoise: A Trickster Tale From the Amazon*
    by Gerald McDermott, (2005) Macmillan

  - *Just in Case: A Trickster Tale and Spanish Alphabet Book*
    by Yuyi Morales, (2008) Macmillan

  - *Trick of the Tale*
    by John & Caitlin Matthews, (2008) Candlewick

  - *Trickster Tales: Forty Folk Stories From Around the World*
    retold by Josepha Sherman & David Boston (illus.), (1996)
    August House

  - *Zomo the Rabbit: A Trickster Tale From West Africa*
    by Gerald MeDermott, (1996) HMH

NOVEMBER: THANKSGIVING

- **Books**
  - *Balloons Over Broadway: The True Story of the Puppeteer of Macy's
    Parade*
    by Melissa Sweet, (2011) Houghton Mifflin

- *Duck for Turkey Day*
  by Jacqueline Jules & Kathryn Mitter (illus.), (2009) Albert Whitman & Co.

- *Gracias, the Thanksgiving Turkey* (English and Spanish editions)
  by Joy Crowley, Maryam Muhammad Abdullah, & Joe Cepeda (illus.), (2005) Scholastic

- *Grandma's First Thanksgiving*
  by Michelle Mensore Condon, (2013) Montani Communications

- *How Many Days to America?: A Thanksgiving Story*
  by Eve Bunting & Beth Peck (illus.), (1990) Houghton Mifflin

- *Molly's Pilgrim (Jewish)*
  by Barbara Cohen & Daniel Mark Duffy (illus.), (1998) HarperCollins

- *Millie and the Macy's Parade*
  by Shana Corey & Bret Helquist (illus.), (2006) Scholastic

- *Rivka's First Thanksgiving*
  by Margaret Okon Rael & Maryann Kovalski (illus.), (2001) Simon & Schuster

- *1621: A New Look at Thanksgiving*
  by Catherine O'Neill Grace, Sisse Brimber, & Plimoth Plantation, (2004) National Geographic Society

- *Squanto's Journey: The Story of the First Thanksgiving*
  by Joseph Bruchach, (2007) HMH

- *Thanksgiving and Other Harvest Festivals*
  by Ann Morrill, (2009) Infobase/Chelsea House

- *The Thanksgiving Door*
  by Debby Atwell, (2006) HMH

DECEMBER FESTIVALS OF LIGHT

See Amazon children's books: Multicultural Christmas (many books)
See Amazon children's books: Hanukkah (many books)

- **Books**
  - *The Boy Who Found the Light: Eskimo Folktales Retold and Illustrated With Wood Engravings*
    by Dale Dearmond, (1990) Sierra Club

  - *Eight Candles to Light: A Chanukah Story*
    by Jonny Zucker & Jan Barger Cohen (illus.), (2001) Barron's Educational Series

- o *Feast of Lights*
  by Ellen Jaffe, (2006) Sumach

- o *Lanterns and Firecrackers (A Chinese New Year Story)*
  by Jonny Zucker & Jan Barger Cohen (illus.), (2014) Barron's
  Educational Series

- o *Light the Lights! A Story About Celebrating Hanukkah and Christmas*
  by Margaret Moorman, (1999) Scholastic

- o *Lighting a Lamp: A Diwali Story*
  by Jonny Zucker & Jan Barger Cohen (illus.), (2004) Barron's
  Educational Series

- o *Nine Days to Christmas: A Story of Mexico*
  by Marie Hall Ets & Aurora Labastida, (2014) StarWalkKids

- o *Premlata and the Festival of Lights*
  by Rumer Godden & Ian P. Andrew (illus.), (1999) HarperCollins

- o *The Spider's Gift: A Ukranian Christmas Story*
  by Katya Krenina, (2010) Holiday House

- o *Together for Kwanza*
  by Juwanda G. Ford, (2000) Random House

- o *Tree of Cranes*
  by Allen Say, (2009) HMH

- o *Yin Li's Lantern: A Moon Festival Tale*
  by Brenda Williams & Benjamin Lacombe (illus.), (2012) Barefoot

- o *Feast of Lanterns*
  by Alan Say, (1976) HarperCollins

- o *Celebrations of Light: A Year of Holidays Around the World*
  by Nancy Luenn & Mark Bender (illus.), (1998) Atheneum

- **Article**
  - o "Diwali"
    http://kids.nationalgeographic.com/explore/diwali/#india-diwali.jpg

JANUARY: NEW YEAR

See Amazon Books for Children: Chinese New Year (many books)

- **Books**
  - o *The Dragon Dance: A Chinese New Year*
    by Joan Holub & Benrei Huang (illus.), (2003) Puffin

  - o *Happy New Year*
    by Emery Bernhard & Durga Bernhard (illus.), (1996) Dutton

- *Happy New Year Everywhere*
  by Arlene Erlbach, (2000) Millbrook Press

- *Lanterns and Firecrackers: A Chinese New Year Story*
  by Jonny Zucker & Jan Barger Cohen (illus.), (2014) Barron's Educational Series

- *New Years' Day (True Books: Holidays)*
  by Dana Meachen Rau, (2000) Children's Press

- *Shanté Keys and the New Year's Peas*
  by Gail Piernas-Davenport & Marion Eldridge (illus.), (2007) Albert Whitman

- *Ten Mice for Tet*
  by Pegi Deitz Shea, Cyntia Weill, & Ngoc Trang (illus.), (2003) Chronicle

- **Recipe**
  - Recipe and history for New Year's Southern "Good Luck Hoppin' John"
    http://whatscookingamerica.net/History/HoppinJohn.htm

FEBRUARY: WAYS TO SAY I LOVE YOU

- **Books**
  - *A Chair for My Mother*
    by Vera B. Williams, (2007) Greenwillow

  - *Each Kindness*
    by Jacqueline Woodson & E. B. Lewis (illus.), (2012) Nancy Paulsen Books

  - *Everyone Says I Love You*
    by Beegee Tolpa, (2010) Price Stern Sloan

  - *The Friendship*
    by Mildred D. Taylor & Max Ginsberg (illus.), (1987) Dial (1997) Puffin (Kindle Edition)

  - *The Giving Box*
    by Fred Rogers, (2000) Running Press

  - *How My Parents Learned to Eat*
    by Ina R. Friedman & Allen Say, (1987) HMH

  - *How Far Do You Love Me?*
    by Lulu Delacre, (2013) Lee & Low

  - *A Kiss Means I Love You*
    by Kathryn Madeline Allen, (2012) Albert Whitman

- o *Love as Strong as Ginger*
  by Lenore Look & Stephen T. Johnson (illus.), (1999) Antheneum

- o *Mama, Do You Love Me?*
  by Barbara Joose & Barbara Lavalee (illus.), (1998) Chronicle

- o *One Love (based on the song by Bob Marley)*
  by Cedella Marley & Venessa Newton (illus.), (2011) Chronicle

- o *The Other Side*
  by Jacqueline Woodson & E. B. Lewis (illus.), (2001) G.P. Putnam's Sons

- o *Papa, Do You Love Me?*
  by Barbara Joose & Barbara Lavelee (illus.), (2005) Chronicle

- o *A Smart Girl's Guide to Friendship Troubles*
  by Patti Kelley Criswell, (2013) American Girl

MARCH: FAIRIES AND INVISIBLE PEOPLE

- **Books**
  - o *The Crimson Elf: Italian Tales of Wisdom*
    by Michael Caduto, (1999) Fulcrum

  - o *Finding Fairies: Secrets for Attracting Little People From Around the World*
    by Michelle Roehm McCann, Marianne Monson-Burton, & Davidi Hon (illus.), (2004) Beyond Words

  - o "How Janet Fought Against the Queen of Elves" in book: *Celtic Tales*
    retold by Elena Chmelová, (1987) Exeter

  - o *Makiawisug: The Gift of the Little People*
    by Jane Fawcett, Joseph Bruchac, & David Wagner (illus.), (1997) Little People

  - o *The Menehune and the Nene*
    by Susan Yamashita & Barbara O'Connor (illus.), (1984) Press Pacifica

  - o *The Quinkins*
    by Percy Tresize & Dick Roughsey, (1982) Collins

APRIL: EGGS AND BASKETS

- **Books**
  - o *The Basket Woman: A Book of Indian Tales for Children*
    by Mary Hunter Austin, (2011) Cosimo

  - o *Beauty, Her Basket*
    by Sandra Belton & A. Cozbi, (illus.), (2004) Greenwillow

- o *A Birthday Basket for Tia*
  by Pat Mora & Cecily Long (illus.), (1997) Alladin

- o *The Cherokee Basket Weavers*
  by Theresa DeAngelis & Rachel A. Kiestker-Grack (ed.), (2003)
  Blue Earth

- o *Chicken Sunday*
  by Patricia Polacco, (1998) Puffin

- o "The Egg Prince" in book: *The Starlight Princess and Other Princess Stories*
  by Annie Dalton, Belinda Downes, & Dorling Kindersley Publishing Staff, (1999) DK Publishing

- o *Fiesta!*
  by Ginger Foglesong Guy & Rene King Moreno (illus.), (2003)
  HarperCollins

- o *Hold Everything! (World of Difference)*
  by Sara Corbett, (1996) Children's Press

- o *Kanu's Basket: A Story From Indian Island*
  by Lee DeCora Francis & Susan Drucker (illus.), (2012)
  Tilbury House

- o *Rechenka's Eggs*
  by Patricia Polacco, (1996) Penguin

- o *A Sweet, Sweet Basket*
  by Margie Willis Clary, (1995) Sandlapper

- o *The Talking Eggs*
  by Robert D. San Souci & Jerry Pinkney (illus.), (1989) Dial

MAY: FLOWERS

- **Books**
  - o *Flower Garden*
    by Eve Bunting & Kathryn Hewitt (illus.), (2000) HMH

  - o *The Flower Man*
    by Mark Ludy, (2005) Scribble & Sons

  - o *How a Seed Grows*
    by Helen Jordan & Loretta Krupinski (illus.), (also in Spanish), (2000) HarperCollins

  - o *Planting a Rainbow*
    by Lois Ehlert, (2003) HMH

  - o *A Weed Is a Flower: The Life of George Washington Carver*
    by Aliki, (1988) Simon & Schuster

Yellow Ribbons   4

Interactions Stress Collectivity as Well as Individuality

Here the central question is whether we are educating students in ways that make them responsive to the claims of community upon their lives. Are they simply learning to compete for scarce rewards as isolated individuals, or are they learning how to create communities of abundance in their lives, both as learners and as citizens?

—Parker Palmer, Author, Educator,
Founder of the Center for Courage and Renewal

In many ways, a good and healthy life consists of creating a dynamic balance between our individual identity and our sense of collective belonging. Parker Palmer, a truly visionary educator, has been a mentor for me in this regard. About 20 years ago, I sat with him and a small group of thoughtful teachers in Taos, New Mexico, where we discussed the balance of the Personal and the Communal in educational design. Parker, who emphasizes an "ethical education," pointed out that an overemphasis on the Personal (getting good grades, getting ahead, succeeding on one's own) without experience of genuine community, can lead to a closed, private world of loneliness, confusion, and a distorted sense of self (Palmer, 1993). We can easily see this in the epidemic of depression and suicide among young people in our society and other technologically developed countries that focus narrowly on individualism and educate through arduous competition and high-stakes testing. On the other hand, Parker says, an overemphasis on the Communal aspect, without learning respect for one's unique identity, can lead to a crowd mentality wherein we become people-pleasers, or susceptible to the gang or the clique—the pseudo-community that expects surrender of our individuality to the "groupthink." We know that these kinds of dysfunctional youth groupings are rampant in our times and often fueled by the emotional fallout of those kids who don't feel able to "make it" on the ladder of educational and societal success.

To begin, let us review two more Vertical Threads that can fortify your understanding of the value and purpose of these Yellow Ribbons:

- **The Classroom Is a Community**
  and
- **We Are All Alike and We Are All Different**

Again, review your notes from thoughtful study or discussion of these two premises from the Vertical Threads chapter and keep them in mind as you go through the Yellow Ribbons. Be aware of your thinking and feeling about the value of community and community-building skills in the children's lives and their learning. Go deeply into your understanding of the importance of highlighting both sameness and difference in your approach to life and learning with children. Do you believe that these vertical threads can help in the development of their collective and individual identities? If you are not certain that these things are important, are you willing to try them on for size, just to see if they grow on you? Pay attention to how your opinions and attitudes about these two Vertical Threads might be resistant, amenable, or shifting as you proceed in your thoughtful reading and your collegial conversations. Holding these two Vertical Threads in mind, let us consider the ways the Yellow Ribbons emphasize the balance between collectivity and individuality.

Like Parker Palmer, I believe that an equal emphasis on the vectors of the Personal and the Communal must be consciously addressed in educational programs to help students find genuine success and happiness in school and in life. Guided by this awareness, you can do much to reinforce the emotional, social, and mental health of your students by addressing both aspects of their identity. In this chapter, we will focus on three specific avenues to create this balance between collectivity and individuality: *Circle Time*, *Infusion Activities*, and *Cooperative Learning*.

CIRCLE TIME

As mentioned in the Orange Ribbons chapter, a Circle Corner is a most vital ingredient in the design of the culturally responsive classroom.

If you can structure your day so that its beginning and ending take place in the Circle Corner, you will create a nest of circular space and time to exponentially increase your students' sense of community, as well as enhance their perceptions of their own worth as individuals. *Circle Time* is consciously used by the culturally responsive teacher to assure that all students have been seen, heard, understood, connected to others, and given respect from you and their classmates (Clifford, n.d.). In this way, we enhance both the brain and the heart power of our students, thus giving them the sense of safety and confidence necessary for developing good speaking and listening skills. These skills, in turn, will help them meet the Common Core requirements and improve their overall academic performance (Dove & Honigsfeld, 2013). Remember to establish the rules of conduct for this space, which will become intrinsically valued by all, as students come to realize that important things happen in *Circle Time*. As far as what takes place in the *Circle Time*, do things you feel will be fun, stimulating, supportive of your curriculum, reinforcing your classroom management, and enhancing both individual identity and community cohesion. You will find that the time taken for this will not detract from the subjects and standards you are required to teach, because you are setting the tone-and-trust foundation that allows the students to attend to their academic studies with greater comfort, confidence and receptiveness throughout the rest of the day. And in this *Circle Time*, you are also concentrating on creating the capacity for connectedness in the lives of your students that is so much a part of the development of both ethical and academic education.

Sample Activities for Circle Time

Although Susannah was taking medication for her epilepsy, she still had some seizures in school. Her parents informed her principal and her teacher, Angie, of the situation, giving as much information as they could about what to do and how to handle Susannah's episodes. After doing more research on epilepsy, Angie decided to utilize Circle Time in her class to educate her students about the issue and show the class how they could support Susannah when she had a seizure. She began by discussing her own childhood issues with asthma and encouraged members of the class to share physical challenges that they had in their lives, asking if there was anything that the class community could do to help them deal with current ones. When Susannah talked about her epilepsy, Angie encouraged her to tell the class what it was and what she needed from the class if she had a seizure. Over the course of several days, Angie showed the class some YouTube videos about diabetes, asthma, and epilepsy conditions that she knew were faced by some of her students. She chose videos of epilepsy that were designed for students' awareness and showed actual episodes. The class learned some basic first aid for Susannah, turning her on her side, cushioning her head, removing any sharp or hard objects from nearby, timing the seizure, calling 911 if the seizure lasted more than five minutes, and staying with her until the seizure ended. In Circle Time, they did some practice runs (without dramatizing the shaking), having several children play the part of the one needing assistance. By preparing the students in this way, in the circular nest of the class community, Susannah's epilepsy was not seen as scary or weird by the other children, but as an opportunity to be of loving assistance to a classmate. When Susannah's first seizure in the class occurred, the students went into action to care for her safety, and the entire group surrounded her, kindly welcoming her back to consciousness.

Challenges

Allow the students to have opportunities to share their challenges, such as the epilepsy in the story above. Allow them to talk about their concerns and fears and what they would want from the class to support them. Be sure to emphasize the fact that although the challenges are different for each of us, everyone has issues in their lives that are hard to deal with and all of us could use kindness and concern from each other.

Dreams

Share dreams. "Does anybody remember their dreams from last night?" "What was your scariest dream ever?" "What was your happiest?" "Have you ever had a dream in color?"

> See ORANGE RIBBONS RESOURCES [previous chapter]: Addressing the Five Senses: Cultural Music, Games, and Dances.

Songs and Chants

Sing songs, learn chants, assign rhythm instruments, or try some rounds and harmonies. Include all kinds of cultural music for this. Play circle games with rhythms.

Marshmallow Roast

Seat one child (per day) in the middle of the circle and allow each of the other children to say what they like about her. Be certain to lay firm ground rules for only positive comments to be given. Avoid focus on the child's looks or clothing, but concentrate instead on aspects of her personality, character, or behavior that are smart, helpful, kind, thoughtful, imaginative, or in any way beneficial to the class community. "I love the way you sing so beautifully!" is one example, or "I like the way you make us laugh!" In introducing this activity, give sample positive feedback statements to one or two children as models, demonstrating what is appropriate and what kinds of positive things to look for.

Talking Stick

Use of the Talking Stick (or some other object, such as a feather or seashell) is a Native American practice employed by many tribes. It teaches a wealth of communication skills, such as how to speak clearly and thoughtfully, how to honor one's own perspective or "truth," how to respect another's viewpoint without need for either agreement or challenge, and how to really listen. Make a Talking Stick and teach the children the Talking Stick protocol. The Talking Stick's cultural history and directions for making and using it are given in this chapter's Supplement pages (by Carol Locust, PhD, Eastern Brand Cherokee).

Choose any subject from the curriculum, or from current events, and allow each student to give his point of view on the matter. With this practice, you will find your students' communication skills growing immeasurably as they relax in the knowledge that their opinion is welcomed and respected, while they also learn to extend that largesse to others.

See YELLOW RIBBONS SUPPLEMENT: The Talking Stick.

INFUSION ACTIVITIES

As mentioned previously, Culturally Responsive Teaching often has more to do with the manner in which any lesson is taught than with new subject matter to be covered. Infusing your existing lessons, in all subjects, with just a few words or a short activity that illustrates or reinforces the basic assumptions underlying good CRT is sometimes all that is required. Asking yourself, before any lesson, "How can I imbue this lesson with a few of the principles of Culturally Responsive Teaching?" is the first step in implementing CRT throughout the day in the elementary classroom. Following are a few samples of activities that can be infused into any lesson to enhance the framework of balance between individuality and collectivity that is called for in the Yellow Ribbons aspect of this culturally responsive approach to teaching.

Sample Infusion Activities

How Are We Alike?/How Are We Different?

Identify the commonalities and contrast the difference of two subjects: two stories, two dragons, two puppets, two clapping games, or two of anything at all, by asking the students the questions: "How are these alike?" and "How are they different?" Draw a Venn Diagram (two interlocking circles) on the board.

> See YELLOW RIBBONS RESOURCES: Infusion Activities: Venn Diagram.

In the space where the circles intersect, write, or have the students write, the similarities between the objects of discussion. Then list the differences in the spaces of each circle that are not overlapping. No matter what subject this activity focuses on, it fosters the underlying premise that similarities and differences in this world are both valuable and worth noting. This is a fundament for appreciating both the unique qualities and the shared commonalities among people of all cultures.

My Side of the Circle

When the students are seated in a circle, ask one child to name five things she sees from her side of the circle (the window, the bulletin board, etc.). Then go to a child on the exact opposite side of the circle and ask him five things that he sees, which will be different (the clock, a classmate, the bookcase, etc.). Now ask the whole group if these two students saw the same things. (Of course, their answer will be "No!") Next, ask the group: "Who was right?" (They will answer something to the effect that they were both right.) "Well, how could they both be right if their answers were different?" you ask. Develop the dialogue along these lines. I have found that even little kindergartners can comprehend this at their level: "They couldn't see the same thing because they were sitting in different places!" With older children, you can plumb the depths of meaning more deeply, discussing how opinions, preferences, habits, and perceptions—the way we each see the world—are all the results of differing points of view, and those points of view are developed by the influences, experiences, choices, people, and environments in our lives. Differences make a difference; they don't have to be seen as right or wrong, just different!

Hundreds of Answers

You can teach almost any subject, skill, or technique with an approach that seeks and elicits not only one right answer but "Hundreds of Answers," as discussed in "Stringing the Vertical Threads." This focus on multiple perspectives engages the whole brain that enjoys the multiplicity of possibilities in life and can entertain many solutions to a question or a dilemma. This is a stance that we and our students would do well to develop, not only to establish more harmonious relationships with others but to access our greater intelligence and to discover creative solutions to the challenges of life. It is a foundation for appreciating the differences that cultures bring to the collective society. Here are two sample subjects in which "Hundreds of Answers" can be incorporated:

Hundreds of Answers

Hundreds of Answers in Math

There are a variety of ways to find an answer to almost any math problem.

While demonstrating a math skill, such as "carrying" in addition, for instance, show the students how it is done with several different processes, or algorithms, to arrive at the same end (Wright Group/McGraw Hill, 2008). Waldorf schools have a most enjoyable approach to math and are particularly noted for using algorithms (Fairman, 2010). Now, ask if anyone has even another way they think we could add big numbers together? Some students may suggest counting objects. Some young mathematicians may suggest adding up the ones first, then those numbers in the tens column, then those in the hundreds, and finally adding all those up together. Even if no one has a suggestion or if some suggestions cannot possibly arrive at the correct answer, you have set the stage for creative thinking and the mutual search for possibilities. This exercise need not be done for every math lesson, but introducing it now and then will make a memorable impression.

See YELLOW RIBBONS RESOURCES: Infusion Activities: Hundreds of Answers.

Hundreds of Answers in Spelling

The words we spell today have only been fixed in recent times. For your own enjoyment and information, read Bill Bryson's book, *The Mother Tongue* (1990). You can show the students how people used to spell *busy* as *bizzy* and *bury* as *berry* which was often more phonetically correct than today's accepted spellings. Every now and then, before a spelling lesson, point out a word, such as *colonel,* that is just not "following the rules" and play with other possibilities that would make that word more "well-behaved." Allow the students to come up with their own contributions before settling down to memorizing the current correct spelling. Tell them that languages are

(Continued)

(Continued)

fluid and changing and that there are many languages that have been absorbed into and used frequently in the English language. Foods are a good way to demonstrate this. Pizza, hamburger, teri-yaki, tamale, and gyros are familiar words to many children. Ask the class if any of them know a word from another culture that is used frequently in English today, opening the opportunity for certain students to volunteer examples from their first language.

Explain that the way we currently spell a word may not be very logical, but is an agreement certain people (like dictionary writers) have made along the word's journey. The students can understand that the generally accepted form still needs to be learned for effective communication in reading and writing.

These activities and discussions are liberating for the mind, offering significant examples of the multiplicity of answers to our questions and setting a stage for greater openness to diversity. Once again, it is not necessary to overdo these activities. But by directly teaching this concept of "Hundreds of Answers," from time to time, you open the way to challenge your students, in any area of study, to see a larger picture of reality than that which offers only right or wrong possibilities.

COOPERATIVE LEARNING

One of the most effective approaches to Culturally Responsive Teaching is the use of *Cooperative Learning* strategies. Students in well-designed groups, organized by an informed teacher, learn invaluable skills of working collaboratively, as well as developing personal responsibility and self-reliance. It has proven to be effective for all types of learners, including mainstream, academically gifted, and ESOL students. Among students with many different ability levels, you will see them developing the capacities for positive interdependence, individual accountability, good communication, leadership, decision-making, conflict resolution, and self-awareness—skills that more and more businesses and business schools identify as basic skills for productive work environments. In the arena of cognitive development, within all areas of the curriculum, comprehensive studies have shown that *Cooperative Learning* approaches increase academic achievement of students of all ability levels by helping students learn faster and more efficiently, retain more, and have more positive feelings about the learning experience (Orlich et al., 2013). As Elizabeth G. Cohen (2014) says in her book *Designing Groupwork*, *Cooperative Learning* is a method that teaches creative problem-solving and increases oral language proficiency, in concert with keeping students on task in their work and managing instruction of students with a wide range of academic skills.

These claims proved consistently true in my classes. With such a plenitude of positive results, you cannot go wrong in adopting *Cooperative Learning* strategies, *if* you are well prepared to do so. Furthermore, when you consider that many of your students come from cultures that place high value on the group and the well-being of all its members, you serve to help them appreciate and capitalize upon what comes quite easily and naturally for them (Gay, 2006).

More individualistic students learn the above-mentioned social skills and the benefits of sharing their ideas and talents with others. They also learn about reciprocity, the awareness that the success of their group depends upon the successful work of each individual within it.

The true benefits of *Cooperative Learning* are dependent upon thorough understanding of the principles and very explicit designs for groupwork (Gillies, 2007). Each member learns the protocol for his specific task, which has been taught in increments. Balanced design of the group is also essential, and placement of hyperactive children, slow learners, or students who distract other students for attention must be carefully considered. There are many basic and advanced cooperative strategies that can be utilized, such as the following:

- Think-Pair-Share: Students have time to think about a problem individually, then work in pairs to solve it and, finally, to share the results with the class.
- The Roundtable: Students sit in teams, taking turns drawing, pasting, or writing one answer to a question.
- The Jigsaw: One student from each team is the expert who goes to other teams to get information and brings it back to his team.
- The Gallery Walk: Students explore a variety of texts or images that are placed around the room, then record or discuss their impressions.

These and other exemplary methods are readily available online, such as those listed and described in an article by Colorin Colorado (2007), entitled "Cooperative Learning Strategies." Each of these structures has its own specific protocols.

The following example demonstrates a *Cooperative Learning* lesson in a culturally responsive fourth-grade classroom. Each student in the cooperative group is given a unique and significant job to do for the group's success, thus reinforcing the idea that one's individuality is important and valuable, as is the well-being of the entire group. The basic skill presented here is the identification of parts of friendly letters and envelopes. In this hypothetical case, you have already assigned the children to heterogeneous groups for the week (or month), taking into account multiple ability levels, male/female balance, as well as cultural and linguistic diversity. Assume that you have already established cooperative norms for groupwork in the classroom. Students have been sequentially prepared for and are familiar with the roles they are to play. Now, having accessed pen pals for them, you have designed a lesson for them to use the friendly letter format to write letters to peers in Nicaragua.

See YELLOW RIBBONS RESOURCES: Cooperative Learning: Pen Pals.

Sample of Cooperative Groupwork

Class Demonstration

Give a class demonstration, using a docucam, naming the parts of the letter and of the envelopes, perhaps using a rhythmic call-and-response format to help students identify and memorize the different parts of the letter. Question, in rhythm: "What do we call this part of the letter?" Answer, in rhythm: "This is called head-ing!" (More information on Call-and-Response teaching strategies will be given in the Green Ribbons chapter.)

Student Practice

Allow students to practice the placement of their names, addresses, dates, and greetings on individual practice sheets and envelopes. Be prepared with the significant data for those students who may not yet know their addresses. Have them save these forms for the next step in groupwork.

Clarify Group Tasks

Now, with work stations or desk arrangements already established, give groupwork tasks, with clear verbal directions for the group that are also written on paper. Today's task is to design the format for letters to a group of Nicaraguan pen pals: The Heading, the Greeting, the Complimentary Close, and the place for the Signature. (Tomorrow the group will design the body of the letters.)

Assign Roles

Publicly assign each member of the group a role for this day's activity, and clearly give them the authority to act in this role for this particular task. Specify exactly what this role will be and make sure everyone knows what each role player is supposed to do. At this point, if the preparation for groupwork has been thorough, the group would be able to work independently, and recover from any mistakes, without the teacher.

The Facilitator

. . . reads the directions aloud to the group and asks if everyone under-stands what is to be done. She shows the group the name and address of its Nicaraguan pen pal class, then puts the card down and directs the Materials Manager to do his job.

The Materials Manager

. . . secures writing paper with lines designating the various parts of the letter; a large envelope, also with lines designating the placement for addresses; pens or pencils; note cards; and crayons for the task. He also gives each member of the group a role badge to wear: Facilitator, Mate-rials Manager, Translator, Scribe, Clean-Up Manager, and Reporter.

Individual Tasks

Each member of the group writes the information needed on the letter form (referring to the practice sheets from the class demonstration). Then each draws a colorful picture of himself on the note card to accompany the letter. Any questions regarding directions can be asked of the Facilita-tor. Those questions she cannot answer are taken to you, the teacher. She is the only member of the group to come to you.

The Translator (perhaps assigned this task because of her fluency in Spanish)

. . . can show the group how to say and write a greeting in Spanish alongside of the English greeting. (This would be *Hola* or *Buenos Dias,* but allow the student to be the expert.)

The Scribe

. . . addresses the envelope with the help of the group.

Further Facilitation

The Facilitator makes sure everyone has finished his task before moving on to the next step. When the group has completed the task, the Facili-tator asks the group some concluding questions. These can be designed and demonstrated by the teacher at the beginning of the groupwork session or can originate from the Facilitator herself if she and the group are experienced with the process: "Are you excited about hearing from our Nicaraguan pen pals?" or "Did you enjoy this assignment?" or "What are you looking forward to learning about our pen pals?"

The Clean-Up Manager

. . . asks each person to do a cleaning assignment: Gather the papers, cards, and envelopes in a neat pile for tomorrow's assignment; put away

(Continued)

(Continued)

the crayons and pens; rearrange the desks; or whatever is needed and expected in the classroom protocol.

Reflection

The Facilitator helps the group reflect on its process and progress. The use of student rubrics and checklists would be helpful in doing groupwork, containing such questions as: Did we give eye contact to the speaker? Did we disagree respectfully? Did everyone contribute to the group? This is an opportunity for individual group members to self-evaluate how they supported the group's learning process. Teach them to avoid "naming or blaming" or focusing on other individual students, but to focus instead on their own helpful participation and the group's success as a whole.

The Reporter

. . . makes an oral report to the whole class based on the group's suggestions and his own perceptions of the group's successful completion of the task.

You can see that quite a bit of preparation time is needed for group tasks if your *Cooperative Learning* is to be successful. But the ability of the groups to work independently develops quickly with a good foundation of clear expectations and well-defined protocol. You will find that as their dependence upon you for continued direction decreases, you will be more and more relaxed with this strategy and have extra time for valuable observation of your students. It is optimal to introduce the basic procedures and roles slowly over time, starting with groups of two, in the beginning of the year. Then you can gradually move to groups of three, four, five, even six, introducing the different kinds of roles as familiarity and confidence in the process develops.

You have probably noted that this particular lesson was *infused* with several aspects of CRT. The fact that the letters are going to children in a Spanish-speaking country, and that such exchange and development of friendships in another country will give your students more understanding of the diversities in the world, is one such aspect. The opportunity for one member of the cooperative group to share her knowledge of Spanish without being too singled out for attention is another CRT *infusion* into the lesson. But beyond these obvious ones, the very use of the *Cooperative Learning* teaching approach is, in itself, good CRT methodology. It is a strategy that is comfortable for children from many different cultures that have a strong communal focus and teaches all your students to work together with respect, gaining the multiple social and academic benefits of community and good group synergy.

It should be emphasized that *Cooperative Learning* does not need to be used for every lesson, for there are many times when individualized instruction, homogenous groups, and whole class instruction are more appropriate and children have different individual preferences for the various instructional modes. But as mentioned, there are so many benefits of *Cooperative Learning*, especially for culturally diverse students, it behooves you to utilize this strategy frequently in your creative CRT. If you have been using *Cooperative Learning* strategies before now, then you are already applying an important aspect of CRT.

Although the *Cooperative Learning* approach is relatively simple once it is established, its success requires careful planning in the beginning. It is essential that you prepare yourself well and systematically. Doing it justice is not within the scope of this book, and I encourage you to avail yourself of good resources for *Cooperative Learning* structures and strategies (Johnson & Johnson, 2009; Johnson, Johnson, & Halubec, 2007).

Although *Cooperative Learning* has been a defined learning modality for almost 20 years, not all teachers have been able to benefit from its use, from a dearth of exposure to its theory and practice, from a lack of thorough understanding of its benefits and strengths, or from inadequate preparation of the students. But for the Yellow Ribbons aspect of CRT, I encourage you to immerse yourself in learning as much as possible about its application, or continuing to improve your existing knowledge, because *Cooperative Learning* truly offers an exemplary, balanced interplay between collectivity and individuality in your students' education.

Furthermore, it is important to add that your cooperation as a team member of the staff in your school is not only a wonderful model for your students but can be a source of great inspiration, creativity, and support for you. As Mara Sappon-Shevin (2010) says in her book, *Because We Can Change the World*, "It is very hard to ask teachers to create inclusive, supportive, and cooperative classroom communities when they themselves do not feel valued and supported" (p. 24). With this in mind, consciously address your own and other teachers' needs for community by cooperatively planning with members of your grade level, with the librarian, the P.E. teacher, the music teacher, and other members of your staff. You also deserve to benefit from this effective approach to life and learning.

As demonstrated here, there are many ways to enhance the healthy balance between Collectivity (the Communal) and Individuality (the Personal) in your classroom. *Circle Time* is valuable because it establishes a strong experience of one's unique worth within the context of the supportive community. *Infusion Activities* clearly demonstrate the balance of uniqueness and commonality in all areas of skill development. *Cooperative Learning* structures and procedures teach the skills of how to be responsible, both independently and interdependently within a group. Hopefully, you will find these approaches to be valuable strategies for CRT. Gently absorbing any one of these into your teaching style will draw you into an increasingly more rewarding experience of your classroom community. For each step you make in this direction, I know that you and your students will find great returns in both affective and cognitive development.

YELLOW RIBBONS

QUESTIONS TO PONDER AND DISCUSS

Utilize these questions for personal reflection or group discussion with colleagues.

- What is your response to Parker Palmer's quote at the beginning of this Yellow Ribbons chapter?
- What do *you* believe is the central purpose of education?
- How would you define "community"?
- Why is community important in the educational process?
- What are some of your ideas for fostering the sense that *The Classroom Is a Community*?
- How would you define "individuality"?
- Why is a child's sense of individuality important in living and learning?
- What are some of your suggestions for honoring the unique individuality of each of your students?
- How does the Yellow Ribbons' focus upon Collectivity and Individuality match with your experience of school as a student from kindergarten through college?
- In these two categories of Collectivity and Individuality, what do you wish you had more of? Less of?

- How does the Vertical Thread of "**We Are All Alike and We Are All Different**" apply to the Yellow Ribbons precept that interactions in the classroom should stress collectivity as well as individuality?
- Do you consider *Circle Time* to be an important element in your daily class structure? If you already use it, what are its benefits? If you do not use it yet, can you see *Circle Time* as a valuable teaching strategy? If so, why?
- Have you ever used a Talking Stick? If so, what was your experience?
- What are the benefits that you see for using a Talking Stick with your students?
- Give an example of a normal lesson, in any academic subject, that you will be teaching at your grade level. Suggest an Infusion Activity that will weave CRT into the way this lesson is usually taught.
- Have you ever been taught within a *Cooperative Learning* classroom or used *Cooperative Learning* techniques with your own students? What worked for you? What did not work? Discuss aspects of why it did or didn't work?

YELLOW RIBBONS RESOURCES

(All resources available at Amazon.com
unless otherwise indicated.)

INFUSION ACTIVITIES

VENN DIAGRAM

www.eduplace.com/graphicorganizer/pdf/venn.pdf

HUNDREDS OF ANSWERS

- **Books**
  - *How Many Ways Can You Make Five?*
    by Sally Anderson, (2012) Gryphon House
  - *Many Ways to 100*
    by Betsy Franco, (2002) Yellow Umbrella
  - *Size: Many Ways to Measure*
    by Michelle Koomen, (2001) Capstone

COOPERATIVE LEARNING

PEN PALS

www.studentsoftheworld.info

YELLOW RIBBONS SUPPLEMENT
THE TALKING STICK

History

By Carol Locust, PhD
Native American Research and Training Center
Tucson, Arizona
(Tribal Affiliation—Eastern Band Cherokee)

"The talking stick has been used for centuries by many American Indian tribes as a means of just and impartial hearing. The talking stick was commonly used in council circles to designate who had the right to speak. When matters of great concern came before the council, the leading elder would hold the talking stick and begin the discussion. When he finished what he had to say, he would hold out the talking stick, and whoever wished to speak after him would take it. In this manner, the stick was passed from one individual to another until all who wished to speak had done so. The stick was then passed back to the leading elder for safe-keeping. Some tribes used a talking feather instead of a talking stick. Other tribes might have a peace pipe, a wampum belt, a sacred shell, or some other object by which they designated the right to speak. Whatever the object, it carries respect for free speech and assures the speaker he has the freedom and power to say what is in his heart without fear of reprisal or humiliation. Whoever holds the talking stick has within his hands the sacred power of words. Only he can speak while he holds the stick; the other council members must remain silent. The eagle feather tied to the talking stick gives him the courage and wisdom to speak truthfully and wisely. The rabbit fur on the end of the stick reminds him that his words must come from his heart and that they must be soft and warm. The blue stone will remind him that the Great Spirit hears the message of his heart as well as the words he speaks. The shell, iridescent and ever changing, reminds him that all creation changes—the days, the seasons, the years—and people and situations change, too. The four colors of beads—yellow for the sunrise (east), red for the sunset (west), white for the snow (north), and green for the earth (south)—are symbolic of the powers of the universe he has in his hands at the moment to speak what is in his heart. Attached to the stick are strands of hair from the great buffalo. He who speaks may do so with the power and strength of this great animal. The speaker should not forget that he carries within himself a sacred spark of the Great Spirit, and therefore he is also sacred. If he feels he cannot honor the talking stick with his words, he should refrain from speaking so he will not dishonor himself. When he is again in control of his words, the stick will be returned to him."

Requests for more information about the Talking Stick will be forwarded to Dr. Carol Locust. Please send requests to comments@acaciart.com © 1997–2007 Acacia Artisans ®

How to Make a Talking Stick

Find a sturdy, but lightweight stick that can be easily handled and passed among the students. Carve it, paint it, or wrap it with yarn and hang shells, feathers, beads, or other objects of meaning or import upon it.

Benefits of the Talking Stick

- Since it honors Native American tradition, it establishes in the minds of the students the teacher's respect for the gifts of other cultures.
- It fosters good communication giving each student a chance to speak and to speak "from the heart" or from one's own understanding of what is true.
- Similarly, the Talking Stick protocol gives the message to the students that each person's contribution is genuinely valued and solicited for the benefit of the whole class.
- When the Talking Stick is used frequently, it teaches the art of thinking for oneself and being able to articulate those thoughts without fear of rebuttal.
- It teaches students how to genuinely listen to each other (a much needed skill in today's world) in order to receive others' contributions without the need for agreement, judgment, or response.

Rules of the Talking Stick

- Speak only when the object is in your hands.
- Speak from your heart.
- Try not to think ahead of time about what you want to say. Allow your contribution to be spontaneous and true.
- Don't ramble. Allow time for others' turns.
- Listen from the heart, too.
- You are not required to speak when the stick comes to you. But when the stick has passed around the completed circle, you may choose to speak then.
- You *are* requested to pay attention and *be* here.

©iStockphoto.com/Susan Chiang

Green Ribbons   5

Students Are Affirmed in Their Cultural Connections

[Successful teachers in a culturally diverse society] see all students, including children who are poor, of color, and speakers of languages other than English, as learners who already know a great deal and who have experiences, concepts, and languages that can be built on and expanded to help them learn even more. They see their role as adding to rather than replacing what students bring to learning.

—Maria Villegas and Tamara Lucas
Preparing Culturally Responsive Teachers

You can see, by now, how interdependent and multilayered are the ribbons you weave for Culturally Responsive Teaching. It could be said that everything discussed in the preceding chapters has also supported the Green Ribbons of affirming cultural connections. As you have attended to making yourself and your classroom invitational and as you have worked toward emphasizing collectivity as well as individuality, you are establishing a culture-safe and culturally affirming environment for your students.

In this chapter, we will discuss three additional ways to affirm your students' ethnic connections and address their cultural dispositions within the lessons you are already required to teach. The first approach is that of *Culturally Inspired Teaching Strategies*, the second is *Inclusive Cultural Topics*, and the third refers to tapping *Students' Store of Knowledge*.

Before we address the specifics of the Green Ribbons—affirming students in their cultural connections—I would like you to review the following Vertical Threads:

- **We Are All American Plus**
  and
- **Every Child Is Gifted**

How does this first concept relate to your previous understanding of what it means to be an American? Do you appreciate the fact that all of us have a variety of cultural identities within our American identity? Regarding the giftedness of every child, are you able to expand your notions of "giftedness" to notice, include, and appreciate the personal and cultural attributes that each of your students brings to the learning community? As you go through this chapter, hold these precepts in mind to see how they might influence your attitudes, your methodologies, and your relationships with your students. There will be more questions to ponder and discuss after reading this chapter. But as you consider the Green Ribbons, be aware of how the Vertical Threads **We Are All American Plus** and **Every Child Is Gifted** might help you affirm your students' cultural connections.

Food for Thought

In learning about and addressing the variety of cultures in your classroom, it is important to distinguish between cultures outside of our American borders and those within them. For instance, although some elements of one's culture of origin will remain, the experience of life in Japan is different from that of Japanese-Americans—people whose families have been here for one or more generations and who identify with being American as much as being Japanese. Of course, those students who are first generation immigrants or refugees are making the transition to living here now and could be considered a third category of lived experience as they make the dramatic shift from one culture to another. Do not make the mistake of lumping all those with a certain ancestry into one pot of assumptions about how they experience culture in their lives. Stay open. Observe. Be sensitive and thoughtful about how your students want to be seen and with whom and what they identify.

CULTURALLY INSPIRED TEACHING STRATEGIES

Good CRT is not only culturally *responsive* but culturally *inspired.* That is, it not only takes into account the various strengths, needs, and learning styles of students from different cultures but actually utilizes those cultural styles and approaches to strengthen the educational process for *all* students. We have already discussed two such methods. Some form of Cooperative Learning is the normal learning method in cultures on many continents that place high value on cooperation. The Talking Stick has been a widespread educational and social practice for clear communication among tribes of Native America. Both of these strategies can be wisely utilized by you, not only for the sake of the students coming from these cultures but for initiating effective ways of learning for all students. Following are three more *Culturally Inspired Teaching Strategies* that will be very useful for you.

Sample Culturally Inspired Teaching Strategies

Call and Response

One enjoyable approach, referred to as "Call and Response" was briefly utilized in the Yellow Ribbons chapter. It is based on African American expressive behavior. Here the "caller" (teacher or a student) sends a message to the group in a rhythmical cadence, and the "responders" call back, either repeating the caller's phrase or offering a previously agreed-upon answer. This is an effective way to reinforce individual leadership, group cohesion, and highly spirited learning, as well as to boost memory retention. Resources and a Supplement included at the end of this chapter give detailed information about the history of this cultural practice and describe ways to initiate the Call and Response strategy. Using this technique can lead to your class creating its own chants for supporting a variety of learning objectives.

Qigong

Another strategy that is extremely helpful for students is the use of the Chinese practice of Qigong (pronounced "chee gong") to bring mind and body into alignment and health. The practice does not require athletic ability or muscular strength and can be done by most students, modified for those who have physical challenges.

See GREEN RIBBONS RESOURCES: Culturally Inspired Teaching Strategies: Call and Response.
Also see GREEN RIBBONS SUPPLEMENT: Call and Response.

People of all ages practice this discipline in America as well as China. The exercises are relaxing, tonifying, and balancing to the right and left hemispheres of the brain. Qigong movements are slow, gentle, circular, and oriented to deep breathing and blood circulation. They are simple to learn, but subtly powerful in the ways that they bring balance, calm, and positive emotion into the students' thought processes and behaviors.

(Continued)

(Continued)

Just a few moments in the morning (during Circle Time) or in between academic activities has immense benefit for the children. Qigong helps to calm as well as energize students, improve their health, increase concentration, decrease stress, and reduce aggression. And, of course, Qigong is also bound to stir interest in learning about the cultures of China and Chinese Americans. You can employ the use of a small gong to initiate a short period of Qigong that sets a respectful tone for movement in silence and grace.

See GREEN RIBBONS RESOURCES: Culturally Inspired Teaching Strategies: Qigong.

Storytelling

Storytelling is another *Culturally Inspired Teaching Strategy*—an ancient educational art featured in all cultures. Storytelling is coming back into prominence in western education as a valuable teaching method and powerful communication tool that appeals to children (and the child in all of us). It is proving to be highly effective in conveying information, not only in language arts but in all the subject areas across the curriculum (Gillard, 1996; Norfolk, Stenson, & Williams, 2006; Strauss, 2006). Many students will come into your school environment from cultures that still maintain a thriving and vital oral tradition and will feel very much at home when you bring them into the enchantment of the story.

Children who are more auditory than visual will also benefit greatly when the curriculum comes alive through storytelling. And yet, as with many *Culturally Inspired Teaching Strategies,* these are not the only students who will benefit from this fundamental art of human expression. For all children, the oral story creates interest, relaxation, the opportunity to communicate thoughts and feelings, and to explore new ideas (Stoyle, n.d.). Storytelling is a remarkable contribution to all students' imaginative facilities and critical thinking abilities (Fredericks, 1997), building auditory skills in a world where visual skills prevail. The reading and writing skills of language proficiency are enhanced in the interactive conversations of storytellers and listeners that allow for the communication of thoughts and feelings. The oral vocabulary established through storytelling increases the listener's speaking vocabulary through the poetic use of language and sometimes archaic words. In many ways, too, storytelling is emotionally therapeutic, helping the children deal with their feelings. And just as it has been for children in the cultures of every era and continent, storytelling is a wonderful, nonpedantic method for conveying values and helping them to consider moral issues. With these many advantages, storytelling should be a practice high on the list of those you wish to put in your CRT toolbox.

We live in a time of rich cultural mingling and interchange, and there are many gifts from every culture that can be garnered to deepen and enrich our students' educational experience. A culturally responsive teacher enjoys weaving many methods into her repertoire and is always thinking about possibilities. Watching, amazed, while Tibetan nuns engaged in a dynamic and challenging form of debate that used hand slapping and rhythmic rocking movements to make their points, I wondered how this obviously stimulating and mentally challenging exercise might be applied to the elementary classroom. Observing a Maori man teaching the sacred dances and songs of their culture to the young people under the trees, I wondered about how we could spend more time in nature with our students, teaching them to live with greater beauty and grace in natural settings. *Culturally Inspired Teaching Strategies* come from a mindset that always seeks to learn more about life and teaching from the rich variety of human culture that is now available to us for our learning.

INCLUSIVE CULTURAL TOPICS

The *Inclusive Cultural Topics* approach is an expansion of the use of Universal Monthly Themes, within the Orange Ribbons chapter, that now moves further into the subject areas of your curriculum, having many wonderful benefits. *Inclusive Cultural Topics* is a practice that is not an "add-on" but embeds itself in the standards you are required to meet and the lessons you are already teaching. Furthermore, it does not require becoming an "expert" about other cultures (an impossible task) in order to be a culturally responsive teacher in the subjects you teach. A focus on *Inclusive Cultural Topics* promotes interdisciplinary connections and gives added relish to lessons you are currently addressing. You will see that it is very motivational for your students, improving their learning retention by reinforcing any subject from several doorways of global experience.

The main emphasis of the *Inclusive Cultural Topics* approach is the utilization of comparison and contrast. You have been introduced to this way of thinking in the Yellow Ribbons chapter, where the Infusion Activity "How are we alike? How are we different?" was discussed and the Venn Diagram was suggested as a way to demonstrate the comparisons. That is really the model in a nutshell. I will just expand the possibilities for application here. The essence of this approach is to find a common theme in anything that you are teaching and then to approach this theme from many cultural angles. Once again, the emphasis is on our commonalities as humans as well as our fascinating, enjoyable differences. The introduction of topics can be simple, as in a short discussion during any lesson, or it can be more complex, as in the monthly themes that cradle several subject areas at once.

Inclusive Cultural Reading and Language Arts Topics

The *Inclusive Cultural Topics* strategy takes what children are reading and expands upon the themes. Every story your students encounter in their reading programs will have some universal topic within it. I like to tell my students that "stories have wings," for similar ideas can be found in stories all over the world. The Cinderella story, for instance, is said to be found in 1,500 versions! These variations on topics are wonderful material for writing lessons, dramatizations, and animated discussions. In the Resources section of this chapter, you will find an extensive list of books to address the following *Inclusive Cultural Topics*: Cinderella, Grandparents and Elders, How and Why Stories, Mermaids, Noodleheads, Tooth Tales, and Tricksters.

Don't stop with these, however, but keep discovering *Inclusive Cultural Topics* in all stories. Mistakes and Boo-Boos is a good topic, as is Kindness, or Lost and Found. You will find *Inclusive Cultural Topics* material everywhere when you start looking for them. *Faces* magazine for children is a good resource, focusing as it does on universal themes. You can weave the skill development of other disciplines into these topics, depending upon the amount of energy and time you have. The possibilities are endless, and the lessons are especially invigorating when the students are organized into Cooperative Learning groups.

Sample Activities for Inclusive Cultural Reading and Language Arts Topics

Topics Book Collection

For various activities listed below, see GREEN RIBBONS RESOURCES: Inclusive Cultural Topics: Inclusive Cultural Reading and Language Arts Topics.

Enlist your librarian to help you collect a large assortment of books on a particular topic and make it obvious and available to the students, such as lining the books on a shelf or writing-board tray. Read aloud to the students the story that is most familiar to your class, such as the French version of Cinderella or one in their reading program. Divide the students into smaller groups to read together other stories (one per group) on the same theme. In their groups, have the students compare and contrast the new story with the story you have read or the one in their reading program. Let each group record their ideas on a Venn Diagram (interlocking circle). Have the groups then report back to the class their findings through Venn Diagrams, discussion, dramatization, or written reports.

Variations of Venn

Create a large Venn Diagram for the class with several interlocking circles, discovering what these stories have in common and what are the differences that manifest in the stories.

Writing Stories

Have the students write their own individual or group stories on the topic, utilizing the common threads found in the overlapping portion of the Venn Diagram.

Class Book

Create a large group or class book for each topic.

Topics Art

Decorate the walls and hallways with art projects in cultural styles that depict the topic from those cultural variations.

Topic Festivals

When you discover a popular topic with your students, create a topic festival, such as Festival of Clowns (or Fairies, or Grandparents and Elders, etc.), and spill out into the school or the community, dramatizing or storytelling the variations on the topic.

Topics for Tots

Create opportunities for your students to share contrasting dramatizations with classes of younger students, each group having a story reader or teller and actors. Encourage your students to ask the younger students about the similarities and differences between the stories.

Inclusive Cultural Math and Science Topics

You may not have considered math or science in a cultural context, but these disciplines are rich with cultural perspectives and contributions. It is possible to take many lessons in math or science and point out to the students how these concepts have been developed and utilized by people of other cultures. For older students, be sure to include the contributions that various cultural groups (both within our country and around the world) have made to our understanding of these fields of study. You and your students will enjoy and appreciate the diversity inherent in these subjects, once your eyes and theirs are opened to them. Remember that older students are often interested in primary level picture books that have interesting information. Do not worry about insulting their intelligence by introducing books designed for younger children if the subject fits the theme and supplies them with additional understanding. It is especially fun for them to think of ways to share these books with younger children.

Sample Activities for Inclusive Cultural Math and Science Topics

For various activities listed here, see GREEN RIBBONS RESOURCES: Inclusive Cultural Topics: Inclusive Cultural Math and Science Topics.

Many Ways to Count

For younger students, demonstrate how people count in different languages (as we have already introduced in the Yellow Ribbons chapter) and that different cultures have a variety of ways of holding up their counting fingers.

Counting Devices

Establish a class collection of counting devices, such as stones, dienes blocks, Cuisenaire rods, toothpicks, pine cones, calculators, computers, and counting bears. Include in this collection the Chinese, Japanese, and Slavonic abaci. (You may discover the invaluable use of the abacus for many math lessons for it is a marvelous device to teach counting, addition, subtraction, and place value.)

A Counting Device Story

Read students the story *Knots on a Counting Rope,* about a Navajo grandfather and his grandson. Create this counting rope device with your students and explore ways to use it.

Tangrams Story

To introduce lessons in geometric shapes, use *Grandfather Tang's Story*, which shows how tangrams can be manipulated in a variety of positions to form animals.

Many Cultural Weavers

Study geometric patterns in weavings of blankets and rugs from a variety of cultures. Invite weavers into the class. Do some weaving with the students with either yarn or paper. Discuss the universality of weaving and the many differences of form and materials that are used.

Arabic Numerals and Beyond

Teach older students about the origin of our number system which came from India (technically, Hindu-Arabic numerals) and how numbers are written differently in different cultural systems. (Google: Base Mathematics: Numeral systems by culture.)

A World of Money

Gather a collection of coins and bills from your travels or from friends in other countries. Show the students how money looks different and has different values in different cultures.

Money's Worth

Use the Internet to find exchange rates between the American dollar and the base currency of any country that students want to know about. Keep track of the exchange rates for a period of time on a bulletin board chart. Together figure out how monetarily advantageous or disadvantageous it would be to travel to Mexico or Canada (or anywhere in the world) at any given time.

Global Time Telling

Gather a collection of sundials, water clocks, sand timers, and old fashioned clocks and watches (or collect pictures of these items) to share with the children to introduce a unit in telling time. For older students, teach them to calculate time differences across time zones throughout the world.

Native American Science

Introduce the stories from the Woodland Adventures books, *Spring Planting* and *Fall Gathering,* that offer a different view of science than that of mainstream America. The focus of these books is not so much on dissecting, naming, categorizing, and objectifying the world, as it is on stewardship, good relationship, and a holistic way of understanding the animal and plant kingdoms.

Inclusive Cultural Social Studies Topics

Social Studies, being the study of people, culture, and the various ways we live our lives, lends itself beautifully to CRT, especially if your social studies texts themselves are thematically arranged. You can do a great deal to augment the topics of the text with materials that show and honor the cultural diversity of your students' world, just as in the other subjects discussed here. For younger children, subjects such as Homes and Families, Foods, and Neighborhoods are integral to social studies and lend themselves well to the *Inclusive Cultural Topics* approach. Sample books for Homes and Families are included in the Resources for this chapter.

> See GREEN RIBBONS RESOURCES: Inclusive Cultural Topics: Inclusive Cultural Social Studies Topics: Homes and Families.

For older children, subjects such as Boundaries, Human Rights, and Forms of Government are also conducive to the *Inclusive Cultural Topics* approach. Sample books for Human Rights are also included in the Resources for this chapter.

> See GREEN RIBBONS RESOURCES: Inclusive Cultural Topics: Inclusive Social Studies Topics: Human Rights.

Selected social studies topics are excellent for language lessons as well. The late Tarry Lindquist, a longtime master teacher in Washington state and a colleague of mine on the REACH curriculum design team, organized her entire curriculum around her social studies themes and met her standards and testing requirements in doing so. This may be an approach you will be inspired to adopt if you read her book, *Social Studies at the Center: Integrating Kids, Content, and Literacy* (2000). This would, of course, be a longer term goal. Two additional resources should be mentioned here. One is the *REACH for Kids: Seed Curriculum*, developed by the REACH Center for Multicultural Education. This is a set of K–6 model thematic lesson plans around social studies subjects that incorporate a variety of academic disciplines, building self-esteem and human relations skills, and developing inclusively cultural/global awareness. *Teaching Tolerance* magazine is another resource that offers classroom activities, kits, and handbooks for teachers, many of which are free, to promote topics of goodwill and tolerance among students.

> See GREEN RIBBONS RESOURCES: Inclusive Cultural Topics: Inclusive Social Studies Topics: Further Social Studies Resources.

With the *Inclusive Cultural Topics* approach, you can develop a very comprehensive way to view social studies. This frame of reference will give your social studies lessons and activities a deeper, richer texture. Looking at social studies through this lens highlights the fact that all cultures have gifts and that everyone benefits from friendly interchange between groups. Using the *Inclusive Cultural Topics* approach, the tone of everything you study begins to be less one of learning *about* other people and more one of discovering how connected we are and what we can learn *from* each other. Here, as in all subjects, finding common human themes emphasizes the beauty of the universal aspects of our humanity as well as the diversity we embody.

Inclusive Cultural Art and Music Topics

The arts have always enhanced the learning of most subjects and several suggestions for integrating art, music, and dance into the learning process have been given in previous chapters. Besides enhancing other subjects, however, these areas of study can also provide infinite topics of their own, drawing on rich resources from many cultures and reinforcing many basic skills within language arts, math, and other subjects. Basketry, Kites, Beadwork, Face Painting, and/or Tattoos, Jewelry, Home Interiors, etc. are just a few of the areas of exploration that can be utilized for *Inclusive Cultural Topics* from Art. Drums, Dances, Flutes, and Lullabies are a small selection of those you can use from Music. A sampling of the many resources available for an art theme related to the universal practices of Face Painting and Body Art is provided in the Resource section of this chapter.

> See GREEN RIBBONS RESOURCES: Inclusive Cultural Topics: Inclusive Cultural Art and Music: Face Painting and Body Art.

A list of sources for CDs and books about World Flutes is included as well.

We have so many cultural resources at our fingertips in this Information Age. Utilize your search engine and take advantage of all the publications and materials that are available to you with a modicum of research, and enlist the help of your librarian and your art and music teachers.

> See GREEN RIBBONS RESOURCES: Inclusive Cultural Topics: Inclusive Cultural Art and Music: World Flutes.

When the emphasis is on high-stakes testing and standardization, the arts are often short changed in both time and funding for school districts. But I encourage you to stand strong in making the arts an integral part of your lesson designs, for, as many teachers know, the arts are not only valuable for their own sake in human development but they greatly enhance cognitive learning in academic subjects as well (Tate, 2010). When you consider that many of your students may be predominantly right-brained learners and many others come from cultures where the arts are considered to be staples of the good life and the mark of a well-educated human being, it makes a great deal of sense to utilize artistic expression as a way to make your lessons more meaningful and memorable for your students.

STUDENTS' STORE OF KNOWLEDGE

Affirming your students in their cultural connections relates to the inclusive cultural content of the lessons you teach. But the Green Ribbons have just as much to do with the way in which you bring your students' lives into the lessons through the lens of appreciation for their culture. Tapping their store of knowledge brings kids' actual lived experience into the classroom, takes you into the community, and moves you beyond the arena of cultural awareness into that of cultural engagement. Remembering that students often prefer not be singled out as "Exhibit A" (especially if there are only one or two of them representing a given culture in your class), your invitational manner can become most attractive for them to volunteer knowledge from their cultural backgrounds. Here are some ways to do this:

Drawing on Students' Store of Knowledge

Contributions From Home

Encourage your students to bring in samples from home to augment your monthly or subject themes. As one example among many, students love the Trickster topic (mentioned in the monthly themes of the Orange Ribbons chapter), for almost everyone has tricksters in their cultural repertoire. Potbellied shadow puppets, raven masks, pig pictures, spider stories, coyote tales, and a dad magician found their way into my lessons as the children talked with their parents and grandparents and brought in stories, pictures, artifacts, and family members. A Table Games topic is equally compelling, or one about Pets (where you will learn to appreciate how different cultures feel connected to different animals). The list is truly endless.

Emergent Topics

Watch and listen, and where time allows, let some of what you teach emerge from, or be enhanced by, the children's interests. I remember how a casual first-grade discussion about teddy bears in my classroom evolved into a whole language arts topic of Things We Loved When We

Were Babies. Writing projects included "blankies," "boos" (pacifiers), and cradleboards.

Enriqué brought his dad's beautifully embroidered sombrero to our fifth-grade class. This was far too big for him and caused nearby class-mates to have to look under and over it to see the board, which they did without complaint. We had a "no hats" rule in our school, but I simply could not enforce it on that shy boy volunteering his cultural statement that day! This evolved into a whole study of conversations, written stories, and hat samples from all kinds of places.

Older students might volunteer information on soccer or lacrosse (and invite you to neighborhood games), which could lead to great dis-cussions and research about the rules, the history, the biographies, the politics, etc. of game playing, much of which can be provided by your students. Dancing, music, or any of the arts can bring the students' cultural knowledge into the class, as well as take all of the class out to the community to observe them in their own milieu. Medicine is a great topic of diversity. When they are ill, your students' families may enlist the help of Chinese acupuncturists, Jin Shin Jyutsu practitioners, herbalists, Ayervedic therapists, shamans, *curranderas*, or other tradi-tional healers. Take advantage of what you overhear your students say-ing and go into it, either lightly, in casual discussion, or more in-depth with research and projects that you wrap around the skill standards for any subject.

Artful Questions

Another way to tap your students' cultural knowledge is to ask questions that will elicit it. Questions that are not directed to anyone in particular are often appropriate, such as "Who knows how to count to 10 in another language?" or "Does anyone know a word in another language that means the same as 'window'?" (Students can help you write labels in other languages for different objects in the classroom.) Get in the habit of asking such open-ended questions, encouraging participation and communication: "Does anybody know if the rules for soccer in the United States are the same for every part of the world?" and "It's really hot today. What are the ways your family cools off when it's hot?" Taking off from a math story problem, you could say: "If you were sent to the grocery store, what favorite foods would *you* buy with $10.00?" Then, once they offer their input, follow up with more interested questions: "Wow, that sounds delicious! How do you cook it?" or "That's really interesting! How did you learn that? Did someone in your family teach you this?" Mastering the art of asking questions that show genuine interest and eliciting conversation from your students not only serves to bring forth their enthusiastic contributions but it also models active listening, an important communication skill that, sadly, many people never develop. Hopefully, you will find your students asking similar questions of you and other students, once this becomes a class norm.

Living Family Treasures

Your students' families are a treasure trove of cultural knowledge that can serve you well. Luis Moll says that most "existing classroom practices" both underestimate and limit the intelligence of Latino students. His research at the University of Arizona demonstrates that most families of the Latino community of Tucson had great knowledge that the teachers did not know about and therefore did not utilize to the students' benefit in teaching academic skills. Teachers who learned to create their own social networks of assistance from families and the resources of a community developed a "cognitive resource" for students to thrive in the classroom (Gonzalez, Greenberg, & Velez, 2001). These findings were further replicated with the children and families of New York City, Philadelphia, and Appalachia (Moll, 2014). Moll emphasized that when you approach your students' families carefully and respectfully to learn what they know, they will most likely be more than willing to share their knowledge, their stories, and their skills with your students. How many grandmothers, mothers, or fathers, for instance, know how to weave or quilt (geometry)? Who are the cooks in the family (measuring)? Who in the family knows calligraphy (penmanship)? Who performs spoken-word or does grass dancing (language, music, math, P.E.)? Who is an expert hair stylist (art) or a softball heroine (P.E.)? Who knows the old stories (language arts)? Who sings the lullabies (music)? Who has farming skills (science)? Who knows construction (math)?

It is my belief that there is nothing, absolutely nothing, of interest in a child's life that cannot be utilized as a tool to learn basic skills. Constantly ask yourself: How can I weave this interesting person into today's or tomorrow's skill lessons? Every time you bring in students' family members to demonstrate a skill or share a story, you are enhancing the student's pride in his culture and cultural knowledge, bringing the family and school cultures together, and demonstrating the rewards of your interest, appreciation, enjoyment, and respect for the cultural gifts of all your students.

Simplicity is the foundation for tapping your *Students' Store of Knowledge*, for much of what students and their family members offer comes in candid and unplanned instances. Establishing a graceful rhythm in your daily schedule that allows for such spontaneous moments is most beneficial. Genuine interest and respect elicit much. These things take time and experience to develop. But it need not be

> ## Food for Thought
>
> One of the first steps in valuing your students' cultural identities is to know and value your own. You, too, are a cultural treasure trove of family history, cherished traditions, language, religion, beliefs, preferences, and social expressions. When you are in touch with your own cultural identity, you serve your students in two ways: (1) You become more aware of the fact that you are always expressing the beliefs, experiences, values, attitudes, and assumptions that are linked to your own cultural background and are, thus, more able to modulate your behaviors to accommodate the needs of the students with different backgrounds from your own. (2) Your sharing of your life experiences and your cultural identity builds trust with your students, fostering strong relationships, and inviting their sharing of their lives with you as well (Kennedy-White, Zion, Kozleski, & Fulton, 2005).

complicated. As has been demonstrated here, just the simple inclusion of thoughtful and appreciative questions can capitalize on your students' and their families' caches of cultural wealth, and much can naturally grow from there.

I hope you have gleaned some inspiration in this chapter for how to affirm your students' cultural connections by researching new *Culturally Inspired Teaching Strategies*, by thinking of ways to adopt the *Inclusive Cultural Topics* approach, and by tapping *Students' Store of Knowledge*. As you become more attuned to the depth of your students' personal and cultural lives, you enhance their joy in learning and your joy in teaching, both of which are so essential for academic success. You will discover the additional benefit of relating to your students at ever more authentic levels, finding greater growth and meaning in the time you spend together.

GREEN RIBBONS

QUESTIONS TO PONDER AND DISCUSS

- Discuss *educare* as the root word for "education." Consider the opening quote from the Green Ribbons chapter, regarding the way successful CRT teachers see their role. Write or discuss how you have seen your role as a teacher compared to this understanding.

- Consider and write or discuss your notes on the Vertical Thread, **We Are All American Plus**. How does the metaphor of our American population being more like a "salad bowl" than a "melting pot" fit with your understanding of the Green Ribbons where Students Are Affirmed in Their Cultural Connection?

- Consider the Vertical Thread, **Every Child Is Gifted**. Do you believe this is true? Think of five children that you know and name at least one special gift that this child brings to the world.

- What is the value of introducing *Culturally Inspired Teaching Strategies* to your students of color, or ELL students? Why would you consider it valuable to bring these strategies into the classroom for your students of European ethnicity?

- Can you think of something you have observed in another cultural setting that might be valuable as a *Culturally Inspired Teaching Strategy* for your students? What would that be? What would be its purpose? How would you introduce it?

- Create a teaching demonstration for either your class of students, or your own colleagues, of one of the following activities: "Call and Response," "Qigong," or "Storytelling," involving audience participation. Take time to discuss and evaluate the experience for yourself and those of your audience.

- Choose a lesson you normally teach, or might teach, in any of the subject areas and design it to be an *Inclusive Cultural Topics* lesson with books, music, and other cultural elements to support the topic.

- How does *Students' Store of Knowledge* relate to the root word, *educare*?

- Do you feel enthusiastic about introducing such practices as Contributions From Home, Emergent Topics, Artful Questions, and Living Family Treasures? Why or why not?

- What methods would you like to create to elicit your *Students' Store of Knowledge*?

- Take some time to write about your own "Cultural Bag" as if you were going on a trip and packing all the elements of your cultural influences to take with you. Start with the obvious things like religion, music, dances, foods, holidays, forms of humor, conversational styles, and traditions from your family and community that you enjoy or don't enjoy. Then move into some more subtle aspects of your "Cultural Bag," such as your beliefs about the purpose of life, the things you most value about living, the reason you chose to be a teacher, your understanding of what is proper and improper behavior in public, in school, etc. What is the purpose of education from your cultural background? Conversations with your colleagues can take this exploration to a very deep level when you are willing to genuinely investigate the positive and negative aspects of your own cultural conditioning.

GREEN RIBBONS RESOURCES

(All resources available at Amazon.com
unless otherwise indicated.)

CULTURALLY INSPIRED TEACHING STRATEGIES

CALL AND RESPONSE

- **CD**
  - "Jambo and Other Call and Response Songs and Chants"
    by Ella Jenkins, (1996) Smithsonian Folkways

  - "Multicultural Children's Songs"
    by Ella Jenkins, (1995) Smithsonian Folkways
    and other CDs by Ella Jenkins

  - "Put Your Hand on Your Hip and Let Your Backbone Slip"
    by Bessie Jones, (2001) Rounder Records

- **Book and CD**
  - *Step It Down: Games, Plays, Songs and Stories From the
    Afro-American Heritage*
    by Bessie Jones, (1979) Rounder Records

- **Website**
  - The Cornerstone
    "50 Fun Call and Response Ideas to Get Students' Attention"
    by Angela Watson
    http://thecornerstoneforteachers.com/2014/01/50-fun-call-
    and-response-ideas-to-get-students-attention.html

QIGONG

- **Book and CD**
  - *Chi for Children: A Practical Guide to Teaching Tai Chi and Qigong in
    Schools and the Community*
    by Betty Sutherland, (2011) Singing Dragon

- **DVD**
  - "Qigong 3: Qigong for Kids"
    by Ellie Drew, Institute for Conscious Change

- **Ebook**
  - *Breathe: Tai Chi Qigong for Children and Their Families*
    https://www.facebook.com/BreatheTaiChiQigongForChildren

INCLUSIVE CULTURAL TOPICS

INCLUSIVE CULTURAL READING AND LANGUAGE ARTS TOPICS

- **Magazine**
  - *Faces*
    www.CricketMag.com/Faces

Cinderella Stories

- **Books**
  - *"Catskinella"* in *Her Stories*
    by Virginia Hamilton, (1995) Blue Sky

  - *Cendrillon*
    by Robert San Souci, (1998) Simon & Schuster

  - *The Egyptian Cinderella*
    by Shirley Climo and Ruth Heller, illustrator, (1989) Harper Collins

  - *The Korean Cinderella*
    by Shirley Climo and Ruth Heller, illustrator, (1993) Trophy

  - *The Persian Cinderella*
    by Shirley Climo and Robert Florczak, illustrator, (1999) Harper Collins

  - *The Irish Cinderlad*
    by Shirley Climo and Loretta Krupinski, illustrator, (1996) Trophy

  - *Petronella*
    by Jay Williams and Friso Henstra (illus.), (2000) Moon Mountain

  - *The Rough-Face Girl*
    by Martin & Shannon, (1992) G.P. Putnam

Dragon Stories

- **Books**
  - *The Book of Dragons*
    by Michael Hague, (1995) Harcourt Brace

- o *The Serpent Slayer and Other Stories of Strong Women*
  by Katrin Tchana & Trina Schart Hyman (illus.), (2000) Little, Brown

- **Many Dragon Resources**
  - o See RESOURCES: Orange Ribbons: Universal Monthly Themes: September: Dragons
  - o Google: Dragon Books for Children

Grandparent Stories

- **Books**
  - o *A Beautiful Seashell*
    by Ruth Lercher Bornstein, (1990) Harper & Row

  - o *Grandfather's Journey*
    by Allen Say, (1993) Houghton Mifflin

  - o *Grandma's Purple Flowers*
    by Adjoa J. Burrowes, (2000) Lee & Low

  - o *My Grandma Lived in Gooligulch*
    by Graeme Base, (1988) Penguin Australia

  - o *Just Grandparents: When a Child Is Born, So Are the Grandparents*
    by Bonnie Louis Kuchler, (2004) Willow Creek

  - o *Pablo's Tree*
    by Pat Mora & Cecily Lang (illus.), (1994) Simon & Schuster

  - o *Sitti's Secrets*
    by Naomi Shihab Nye & Nancy Carpenter (illus.), (1997) Alladin

  - o *The Story of the Milky Way: A Cherokee Tale*
    by Joseph Bruchac, Gayle Ross, & Virginia Stroud, (1995) Dial

  - o *Tangerines and Tea*
    by Ona Grines & Yumi Heo (illus.), (2005) Harry N. Abrams

  - o *These Hands*
    by Margaret Mason & Floyd Cooper (illus.), (2010) HMH

  - o *Watch Out for the Chicken Feet in Your Soup*
    by Tomie de Paola, (1974) Alladin

  - o *William and the Good Old Days*
    by Eloise Greenfield & Jan Spivey Gilchrist (illus.), (1993) Harper Collins

HOW AND WHY, MERMAID, NOODLEHEAD, AND TOOTH STORIES

- **Books**
  - o *How and Why Stories: World Tales Kids Can Read and Tell*
    by Martha Hamilton & Mitch Weiss, (2005) August House
  - o *Mermaid Tales From Around the World*
    by Mary Pope Osborn, Paul Werstein, & Troy Howell (illus.),
    (1999) Scholastic
  - o *Noodlehead Stories: World Tales Kids Can Read and Tell*
    by Martha Hamilton & Mitch Weiss, (2000) August House
  - o *Tooth Tales From Around the World*
    by Marlene Targ Brill & Katya Krenina (illus.), (1998) Charles-
    bridge

Trickster Stories

- **Books**
  - o *Anansi the Spider: A Tale From the Ashanti*
    by Gerald McDermott,(1972) Holt Rinehart & Winston
  - o *Coyote: A Trickster Tale From the Southwest*
    by Gerald McDermott, (1994) HMH
  - o *Monkey: A Trickster Tale From India*
    by Gerald McDermott, (2011) HMH
  - o *Raven: A Trickster Tale From the Pacific Northwest*
    by Gerald McDermott,(1993) HarperCollins and more from
    Hawaii, West Africa, and the Amazon by Gerald McDermott
  - o *Lapin Plays Possum: Trickster Tales From the Louisiana Bayou*
    by Sharon Doucet & Scott Cook (illus.), (2011) Pelican
  - o *Love and Roast Chicken: A Trickster Tale From the Andes Mountains*
    by Barbara Knutson, (2004) Carolrhoda
  - o *Porch Lies: Tales of Slicksters, Tricksters, and Other Wily Characters*
    by Patricia Mckissack & Andre Carrilho, (2015) Random House
  - o *A Ring of Tricksters: Animal Tales From North America, the West
    Indies, and Africa*
    by Virginia Hamilton & Barry Mosher (illus.), (1997) Blue Sky
  - o *The Tale of Rabbit and Coyote*
    by Tony Johnston & Tomie de Paola, (1994) Putnam

    ○ *Trick of the Tail*
      by John & Caitlin Matthews, (2008) Candlewick

    ○ *Trickster Tales Around the World*
      by Josepha Sherman, (1996) August House

INCLUSIVE CULTURAL MATH AND SCIENCE TOPICS

Counting

- **Book**
  - *Count on Your Fingers African Style*
    by Claudia Zaslavsky & Wangachi Mutu (illus.), (1996) Writers & Reader

  - *Emeka's Gift: An African Counting Book*
    by Ifeyoma Onyefulu, (1999) Frances Lincoln

  - *Grandfather Counts*
    by Andrea Ange Cheng & Zheng, (2003) Lee & Low

  - *Just a Minute! A Trickster Tale and Counting Book*
    by Yuyi Morales, (2003) Chronicle

  - *Knots on a Counting Rope*
    by John Archambault & Bill Martin, Jr., (1997) Square Fish

  - *Moja Means One: Swahili Counting Book*
    by Muriel & Tom Feeling, (1992) Puffin

  - *The Multicultural Math Classroom: Bringing in the World*
    by Claudia Zaslavsky, (1996) Pearson Education, Canada

  - *Number Words and Number Symbols: A Cultural History of Numbers*
    by Karl Menninger, (1969) Massachusetts Institute of Technology

  - *One Smiling Grandma*
    by Anne Marie Linden, (1992) Dial

  - *One White Sail*
    by S. T. Garne & Lisa Etre (illus.), (1997) Harcourt Brace

Geometry

- **Book**
  - *Grandfather Tang's Story*
    by Ann Tompert, (1990) Crown

Weaving

- **Books**
  - *Abuela's Weave*
    by Omar S. Castaneda & Enrique O. Sanchez (illus.), (1993) Lee &
    Low
  - *Aneesa Lee and the Weaver's Gift*
    by Nikki Grimes & Ashley Bryan (illus.), (1999) Lothrop, Lee &
    Shepard
  - *Geometric Design in Weaving*
    by Else Regensteiner, (1986) Schiffer
  - *Master Weaver From Ghana*
    by Gilbert Ahiagble, Louise Myer, & Nestor Hernandez (photo.),
    (1998) Open Hand
  - *Songs From the Loom: A Navajo Girl Learns to Weave (We Are Still
    Here: Native Americans Today)*
    by Monty Roessel, (1995) Lerner

Money

- **Books**
  - *All the Money in the World*
    by Bill Brittain & Charles Robinston (illus.), (1992) HarperCollins
  - *Apple Picking Time*
    by Michele Benoit Slawson, (1994) Crown
  - *A Chair for My Mother*
    by Vera Williams, (1982) Greenwillow
  - *Chicken Sunday*
    by Patricia Polacco, (1992) Philomel
  - *Erandi's Braids*
    by Antonio Hernandez Madrigal & Tomie de Paola, (1999) G.P.
    Putnam

- ○ *Finders, Keepers?*
  by Elizabeth Crary, (1987) Parenting Press
- ○ *The Gift*
  by Aliana Brodmann, (1993) Simon & Schuster
- ○ *The Gold Coin*
  by Alma F. Ada, (1991) Atheneum
- ○ *My Rows and Piles of Coins*
  by Tololwa M. Mollel & E. B. Lewis (illus.), (1999) Clarion
- ○ *Ox Cart Man*
  by Donald Hall, (1979) Scholastic
- ○ *Pedrito's Day*
  by Luis Garay & Monica Hughes (illus.), (1997) Orchard
- ○ *Project Wheels*
  by Jacqueline Turner Banks, (1993) Houghton Mifflin
- ○ *The Rag Coat*
  by Lauren A. Mills, (1991) Little, Brown
- ○ *The Treasure*
  by Uri Shulevitz, (1978) McGraw-Hill Ryerson
- ○ *Working Cotton*
  by Shirley Anne Wilson, (1992) Harcourt Brace Jovanovich
- **Website:**
  - ○ *www.oanda.com/convert/classic*

Science From a Native American Perspective

- **Books**
  - ○ *The Fall Gathering (Woodland Adventures)*
    by Rita T. Kohn & Winifred Barnum-Newman (illus.), (1995) Children's Press
  - ○ *Spring Planting (Woodland Adventures)*
    by Rita T. Kohn & Robin Scott McBride (illus.), (1995) Children's Press
  - ○ *Keepers of the Earth*
    by Michael Caduto & Joseph Bruchac, (1997) Fulcrum

Inclusive Cultural Social Studies Topics

Homes and Families

- **Books**
  - *Andrew Henry's Meadow*
    by Doris Burn, (2012) San Juan

  - *Families*
    by Ann Morris, (2000) HarperCollins

  - *The Family Book*
    by Todd Parr, (2010) Little, Brown

  - *The Family Under the Bridge*
    by Natalie Savage-Carlson & Garth Williams, (1989) Harper Collins

  - *Houses and Homes*
    by Carol Bowyer, (1978) Usborne

  - *Houses and Homes (Around the World Series)*
    by Ann Morris & Ken Heyman (photo.), (1995) HarperCollins

  - *Two Homes*
    by Claire Masurel & Kady MacDonald Denton, (2003) Candlewick

  - *Wonderful Houses Around the World*
    by Yoshio Komatsu, Akira Nishiyama, & Naoko Amemiya (illus.), (2004) Shelter

Human Rights

- **Books**
  - *Frederick Douglas: Young Defender of Human Rights*
    by Myers & Morrison, (2007) Patria

  - *Mine and Yours: Human Rights for Kids*
    by Joy Berry & Nicole Richardson (illus.), (2005) Powerhouse

  - *We Are All Born Free: The Universal Declaration of Human Rights in Pictures*
    by Amnesty International, (2015) Frances Lincoln

Further Social Studies Resources

- **Books**
  - *REACH for Kids: Seed Curriculum*
    www.reachctr.org

  - *Social Studies at the Center: Integrating Kids, Content, and Literacy*
    by Tarry Lindquist & Doug Selwyn, (2000) Heinemann

- **Magazine**
  - *Teaching Tolerance*
    www.tolerance.org

INCLUSIVE CULTURAL TOPICS: ART AND MUSIC

General Multicultural Art and Music

- **Book**
  - *Art From Many Hands: Multicultural Art Projects*
    by Jo Miles Schuman & Pat Jackunas (contributor), (2003) Davis

- **Many Art Resources**
  - Google children's art by any culture (i.e., Japanese Children's Art)

- **Music CDs**
  - Any of many Putumayo Kids CDs, such as "World Playground"
    and "Dreamland"

Face Paint and Body Art

- **Books**
  - *Body Decoration (Traditions From Around the World)*
    by Jullian Powell, (2003) Thomson Learning

  - *Faces Around the World: A Cultural Encyclopedia of the Human Face*
    by Margo DeMello, (2012) ABC-CLIO

  - *Transformations! The Story Behind the Painted Face*
    by Christopher Agostino, (2006) Kryolan, Berlin

Flutes

- **Books**
  - *The Bravest Flute: A Story of Courage in the Mayan Tradition*
    by Ann Grifalconi, (1995) Little, Brown

- o *The Flute*
  by Rachna Gilmore & Pulak Biswas (illus.), (2012) Acorn

- o *The Flute: A Children's Story*
  by Chinua Achebe, (1977) Fourth Dimension

- o *Flute Lore, Flute Tales: Artifacts, History, and Stories About the Flute*
  by Katherine L. Homes, (2013) Couchgrass

- o *The Flute Player: An Apache Folktale*
  by Lacapa Michael, (1995) Rising Moon

- o *Lady Wenji and the Lament of the Nomad Flute*
  by Heather Clydesdale, (2009) Asia Society

- o *The Song of Six Birds*
  by Renee Deetlef & Lyn Gilbert (illus.), (1999) Dutton

- **Music CDs**
  - o "Crosswinds: World Flute Conversations"
    by Rajenda Taradesai featuring BlueMonk, (2015) Audiobook

  - o "Flutes of the World"
    Various Artists, (2004)

  - o "World Flutes Vol. 1" (various artists)
    (1997) Allmusic

Music and Stories

- **MP3 Download**
  - o *Tamas Flute: New Zealand Maori Stories for Children*
    by Davina Whitehouse

GREEN RIBBONS SUPPLEMENT
CALL AND RESPONSE

History

The "Call and Response" communication pattern is basic to African American expressive behavior, forming the foundation of their collective interactions and relationships. Call and Response is rooted in sub-Saharan African cultures and used in public gatherings to ensure a more democratic process. This pattern of vocal and musical communication is "alive" in the communicative styles of African Americans as seen in a myriad of forms in religious observances, public gatherings, sporting events, children's rhymes, gospel music, rhythm and blues, and jazz. Call and Response is based upon a spoken or sung phrase given by the soloist, followed by an echo or answer pattern from the group. The answer can be given as (1) a verbal or sung phrase, (2) an instrumental response, (3) percussive sounds from the mouth, (4) body percussions of stomping the feet, clapping hands, or slapping knees, thighs or chest, or (5) a combination of any of the above.

Benefits

- By honoring African American traditions, this strategy helps students appreciate the gifts of their own and others' cultures.
- It maximizes individual participation in the life of the group.
- This strategy offers several doorways of multisensory experience to reinforce the learning—synchronizing mind and body in total engagement.
- It gives the students repeated opportunities to lead the group, to improvise, and to develop their own styles in an organized, supportive setting.

How to Use Call and Response in Your Classroom

The listening tapes of Ella Jenkins (listed in the Resources for this chapter) are excellent introductions to Call and Response, giving clear instructions to the listeners as to how to follow Ella's "call." Once the children have had some practice in this form of rhythmical communication, it can be done in many situations and instances to reinforce the learning of the moment or to uplift the students' energy and spirits. In your class, the "caller" (teacher or student) can send a message to the group in a rhythmical cadence, and the "responders" can answer back, either repeating the caller's phrase or offering a previously agreed-upon answer or musical rhythm.

EXAMPLE 1 (WHICH CAN BE ACCOMPANIED BY CLAPPING, MARCHING, OR BODY SLAPPING):

Caller:	"What – is – zero-times-four?"
Class Response:	"Zero-times-four is zer-o."
Caller:	"What – is – one-times-four?"
Class Response:	"One-times-four is fo-ur."

Continue with the rest of the 4-Times Table in the same rhythmic pattern.

EXAMPLE 2:

Caller:	"What day of the week is today?"
Class Response:	"It's Tuesday, the day to be happy."
Caller:	"What day of the week did you say?"
Class Response:	"It's Tuesday, the day to be proud!"
Caller:	"What day of the week is this day of the week?"
Class Response:	"It's Tuesday, the day to enjoy ourselves and to say 'We're smart!' out loud!"

Blue Ribbons 6

Students Are Reinforced for Academic Development

Culturally responsive teachers have unequivocal faith in the human dignity and intellectual capabilities of their students.

—Geneva Gay
Culturally Responsive Teaching Pioneer
University of Washington

Perhaps you were deeply touched by the success of Jaime Escalante, portrayed by Edward James Olmos in the movie *Stand and Deliver.* Against seemingly overwhelming odds, he was able to motivate low-income city kids into levels of academic achievement they never dreamed possible. Over the years, there have been many films of this genre including *Freedom Writers* portraying Erin Gruwell and the made-for-TV Ron Clark Story based on his book, *The Essential 55* (2003). We are affected by such true stories because many of us, as teachers, inherently understand the will, the dedication, and the willingness to break outside of the boxes of convention that good teaching requires. These teachers were willing to do everything within their power to help their students achieve academic success. The truth is that there are thousands of amazing teachers who have not made it into the movies but are working their hearts out every day to help their students overcome such obstacles. I assume that most of these top-notch teachers held a Vertical Thread in their own minds similar to the one we have discussed:

- **Any Student Can Learn Anything**

John is a friend and master principal of a high impact urban elementary school populated by a majority of low-income students of color. When he visited the graduation ceremony at the high school attended by his former students, he was approached by a young woman, who was now graduating with an honors admission to the University of Washington, wanting to thank him for all he had done for her. She said, "You and the teachers at Hawthorne made us think that we were smarter than we thought we were."

As you proceed in this chapter, reread the portion of the Vertical Threads chapter that addresses this assumption that **Any Student Can Learn Anything**. Reflect upon your current beliefs about this Vertical Thread. If it is a bit of a stretch for you, challenge yourself to "try it on" for a while and hold this in the back of your mind while you read of ways to promote the Blue Ribbons. It is a salient assumption in the minds of all good culturally responsive teachers whose students realize great academic victories. We never stop looking for the keys to open each student's intelligence. And because we believe that they can learn almost anything, they usually do.

I hope this chapter will help you take pride in all that you already do and learn even more ways to support your students' success. The Blue Ribbons overlap with the other bright ribbons of the book, for everything designed to address the six other basic principles of CRT also reinforces students' academic development. But here we will focus on four distinct approaches you can use to exponentially increase your students' achievement: *Catch Kids Being Smart*, *Expect the Best From Every Student*, apply *Multiple Modes of Assessment*, and develop a *Positive Rewards System Attentive to Cultural Values*.

CATCH KIDS BEING SMART

The Pygmalion Effect, or the observer-expectancy effect, is the proven theory that the perceptions and expectations of teachers significantly enhance or deter the performance of children (Rosenthal & Jacobson, 2003). In essence, your students become what you believe about them. Capitalizing on this observation, you can increase your students' academic development by creating numerous ways every day to mirror for them their own intelligence. Besides a variety of assessment techniques that you may be using to gather data, guide instruction, and monitor student achievement, the following suggestions are offered as quick-and-easy, informal ways to acknowledge your students' intelligence and giftedness on a daily basis. Remember that you are building a community of trust and support to allow the brain its optimum performance (Hammond, 2015).

Sample Ways to Catch Kids Being Smart

Gleaning Talent

Observe your students constantly, looking for and acknowledging their interest, propensities, talents, and giftedness.

Frequent, Authentic Praise

Praise your students frequently. Avoid criticism while offering critique. Give supportive and clear feedback for improved performance. Find authentic ways to praise each one, at different times (Marzano, Pickering, & Pollock, 2001).

Set-Ups to Shine

Set up situations you know will allow them to shine—to reveal their talents, gifts, and achievements.

Even though he could speak English well enough, Antoin felt anxious about writing because it was not his first language. He showed little interest in the language arts and did not produce assignments in either a timely or a proficient manner. But his fifth-grade teacher, Doug, knew why Antoin was evading the assignments and, believing in his intelligence, kept looking for the portal to his language aptitude in English. He noticed in Antoin a compassion for the little children on the playground and a great penchant for drawing with colored pencils. Doug gave him the assignment to write a picture book for the kids in the first grade, and to write it in French, asking the school's French teacher to help Antoin translate it into English. Since the monthly theme for Doug's fifth-grade class was "Clowns of the World," he asked Antoin to tell the younger children, in writing, about what he had learned on the subject. Antoin's response to that invitation astounded Doug, the French teacher, and the first-grade teacher. He produced a small booklet with colorful, imaginative, multicultural clown drawings accompanied by clever descriptions of the personalities and talents of the clowns. The little children loved the book, delighting in Antoin's visits to their classroom, where he read the book to them in both English and French. Antoin found great pleasure in his accomplishment and wrote several children's books on various topics that year, eventually writing two in English. By close observation, deep interest in his student, and faith in his abilities, Doug had set up the opportunity for Antoin to shine, tapping his genius.

Value Originality

Give as much positive feedback for original thinking as you do for "right" answers.

(Continued)

(Continued)

Praise the Process, Not Just the Results

Acknowledge your students' persistence, eagerness, or curiosity—and any other noticeable qualities or assets.

Reinforce Cooperation

Honor your students for working well with each other or for helping someone who is struggling.

These are just a few of the many ways you can *Catch Kids Being Smart*, and by using them, you will be rewarded with the increased enthusiasm and loyalty they show toward you and toward the process of learning. In this way, you can demonstrate for yourself the positive power of the Pygmalion Effect.

EXPECT THE BEST FROM EVERY STUDENT

In his workshops with teachers, my husband, Gary Howard, often asks participants, "What are the characteristics of the students for whom you are doing a good job?" The teachers' list usually includes things such as good attendance, basic needs met, self-discipline, family that values education. Gary then follows this with: "Looking at your list, would it be fair to say that you are doing a good-to-great job with kids who don't need you that much?" He goes on to say, "The real work of Twenty-First Century school reform is learning to do a good job with the kids who don't come front-loaded for school success."

The demands of the teacher in today's classrooms call for a thorough understanding of the academic standards (what students need to know and to be able to do at each grade level). We have access to a multiplicity of instructional strategies to get our students to meet or exceed these standards (Hattie, 2012). Holding strong to the basic assumption that **Any Student Can Learn Anything**, you will be consistently watching for and using a variety of classroom-based pedagogies and assessments to provide each student with whatever is necessary for optimum academic development. The late Asa Hilliard, writer and brilliant educational psychologist, was once a presenter for an inservice training in my district. I remember how he emphasized that we now have more than enough research data and proven methodologies with which to tap the genius of all our students, but we need the belief, the intention, and the will to use these discoveries in our practice. When a student is not absorbing what you are trying to teach her, when your tried-and-true methods seem to be failing you, then you must turn to the vast amount of research and materials available now in this age of information to find what will work (GLAD, n.d.; Hattie, 2012; Society for Research on Education Effectiveness, n.d.). Never give up trying to tap the aptitudes of each child. Constantly search for the keys to unlock his academic potential. At the same time, you must be realistic and kind to yourself when you have not been able to do the best by each student, for a teacher's days are packed with challenges. But if you adopt the attitude that each student's intelligence is a code to crack, not an insurmountable problem, you will not be falling prey to the tendency to blame the student or her circumstances for her lack of success, which has been a common professional barrier to learning.

Notable culturally responsive educators, Sonia Nieto and Patty Bode, in an article entitled "School Reform and Student Learning" (2013), make a good case for maintaining high expectations and rigorous standards for all learners. They write,

> . . . the difficult conditions in which some students live need not be viewed as insurmountable barriers to their academic achievement. It is too often the case that society's low expectations of students, based on these situations, pose even greater obstacles to their learning. (p. 324)

The wise culturally responsive teacher continually creates opportunities for his students' success. He is clear about grade-level performance requirements from his state and district, which takes the guess work out of his lesson plans. He relies on his knowledge of cultural and individual learning modalities and styles of expression. And he constantly asks self-reflective questions, such as the following:

Sample Questions for Expecting the Best

Atmosphere

Is the material being presented in a respectful, culture-friendly atmosphere (Orange Ribbons)?

Cultural and Individual Styles

Do my strategies and the material I use capitalize on the students' different styles of individual and cultural reception and expression (i.e., enthusiastic verbalization, quiet observation, expressive movement, or group orientation)? (See the Purple Ribbons chapter for further development of this consideration.)

(Continued)

(Continued)

Gradient Steps

Are the lessons taught incrementally, in enough gradient steps for maximum comprehension?

Variety

Do I approach the learning of any skills with persistence and a variety of methodologies? (Again, see the Purple Ribbons chapter.)

Motivation

Are the lessons presented in ways that help my students become independent and interdependent (cooperative) self-motivated learners, inspired by learning itself and gradually less dependent on me as their mediator of knowledge?

Challenge

Am I comfortable with challenging all my students? Do I convey my belief in their ability to master the lessons?

Interesting

Do the lessons stir curiosity and interest?

The motto one should apply to high standards is this: "Never adjust the standards, but continually be modulating the methods by which to achieve those standards." In other words, expect the most from your students, and do your best to help them meet those expectations.

Furthermore, as Asa Hilliard would add, high-stakes testing has nothing to do with high standards. These tests, he claims, are good for companies that make money on testing but are neither appropriate for the diverse groups that make up the country nor for anyone. There is no validated correlation between high standards and the testing being used (Chamberlain, 2004).

MULTIPLE MODES OF ASSESSMENT

Sasha's nimble movements caused the little bells on her skirt to jingle. She wore her long shawl with elegance and dignity, spreading her arms like the wings of a beautiful white bird. Her moccasined feet lightly outlined rhythmic patterns on the earth. Watching her, I was filled with pride for her grace. Sasha showed poor results in math skills on a standardized test in my first-grade class on the reservation. But this day at the powwow I saw her dancing, and later she shyly presented me with the gift of a bracelet she had beaded in beautiful geometric patterns. I knew that the patterns and forms of dance steps and beadwork are integral aspects of the world of mathematics, yet I realized these skills of hers would never be measured by standardized tests. I knew I must find a way to honor and capitalize upon her knowledge.

There are countless cases where it is the test, not the child, that should be questioned. Whose intelligence is being measured here? And how do we define intelligence? I have concluded that most standardized tests do not begin to adequately measure the abilities or the knowledge of most youngsters.

Carol Robinson-Zañartu, an outstanding professor of educational psychology at San Diego State University, told my husband a story about a Native American boy to whom she was administering a multiple choice intelligence test. When instructed to choose a word that most closely corresponded to a picture of a canoe (the choices being sailboat, car, or airplane), he was not able to choose an option, for his knowledge of canoes was too comprehensive to associate them with any of the selections. Instead, he answered, "It looks Ojibwa to me," demonstrating that he not only recognized the canoe but was able to associate it with the construction designs of a certain tribe! The testing protocols would require Carol to record this as a wrong answer. However, in this case, the student was smarter than the test.

On the matter of standardized testing, we need to be valiant in intervening or standing up for our students, for cultural relevance is so important in assessing the abilities and the intelligence of children. Giving them opportunities to demonstrate what they know and what they can do, and using cultural material that is familiar to them is of utmost importance (Hilliard, 2004). Furthermore, we need to deeply consider the detrimental effects on many students from the testing procedures themselves. The essential question to ask is this: Are our forms of assessment building or eroding their confidence in learning (Stiggins, 2006)? If they are eroding confidence, then we should be diligently designing better ways to assess them, lest we interfere with their willingness to learn and nullify our best efforts to teach them.

Being aware of cultural bias included in testing procedures is a big step toward reinforcing academic achievement for your students, because it will lead you to be constantly vigilant to find the ways and means to test them fairly. Let the children, more than the tests, show you how they are smart! Remember that any test is measuring many variables besides the skill it purports to be measuring. Facility with English, experience with this particular mode of testing, self-esteem, fear of success or failure, preferred modes of learning, individual versus group orientation, background knowledge, and familiarity with the stories and test examples, among many factors, influence test taking. When possible, lift out the variable to be tested and see if it can be measured in a range of methods. Multiple forms of assessment are available, depending on what and who is being assessed. And do not forget the value of friendly, supportive conversation. As much as possible, let the kids tell you and show you what they know. Being as explicit as possible, provide feedback to the kids from early stages and throughout a learning process, and then allow them to internalize that feedback in order to articulate what is going well and not so well. This should be our goal in any kind of evaluation (Gardner, 2009). Include in your testing repertoire the following approaches:

Sample Assessment Approaches

Dialogue

Give verbal instructions and then dialogue with the test taker throughout the written test.

Oral and Physical Response

Allow and encourage oral responses (explanations, questions for clarification, descriptions, stories demonstrating understanding) or physical responses (gestures, rhythmic applications, drawings) as well as written ones.

Projects and Performances

Substitute or augment the test with projects (exhibitions and portfolios) or performances demonstrating understanding.

Observation Scales

Learn to develop and use observation scales to evaluate your students' evolving abilities in multiple subjects, identifying a developmental range of behaviors that move toward your goals for them.

Students Goal Lists

At the beginning of the year, help the students create individual goal lists, stated in their words, and outline the steps to attain them. Refer to these frequently and allow the students to put checks or stickers where they (and you) feel that the incremental steps have been adequately achieved.

Cooperative Tests

Through discussion, projects, performances, and reports, test the group for the lessons they have learned together from the material.

Culturally Sensitive Preparation

Be sensitive to the students' unique cultural orientations, values, and approaches to learning when preparing them for standardized testing procedures. (See the Purple Ribbons chapter for more focus on this topic.)

Experience

Make certain that the students have enough experiences with the testing procedure to be fully comfortable with the format.

Access

Be certain that all students are getting the same access to the information. This is especially important for students who may have family problems or obligations that prohibit good attendance, or students who have little time, no resources, and few environments outside of school in which to study and prepare.

Fairness

Continue to reexamine and challenge the emphasis placed on standardized test scores and develop more just and effective alternatives for assessing student achievement, ability, and potential (Ravitch, 2011).

Insist on Equity

Campaign for better, more equitable assessment procedures at the levels of the school, district, state, and nation.

POSITIVE REWARDS SYSTEM
ATTENTIVE TO CULTURAL VALUES

Change was obviously needed in Hawaiian schools when it became evident that by third and fourth grade many Native Hawaiian children had become alienated from school and not engaged in learning. Researchers noted that this demise of enthusiasm and success was the result of an unexamined cultural clash. While Hawaiian children were naturally "gregarious, mutually helpful, talkative, affectionate, and aggressive," these qualities were perceived by their Westernized teachers as "rowdy, restless, inattentive, lazy, and uninvolved." Many modifications were instituted wherein the teachers were trained and coached into taking on a new role with the children. One important aspect was the manner in which the children were reinforced. "Teachers were encouraged to give plenty of praise, hugs, and smiles, and to establish interpersonal ties while still setting forth expectations and rules." With this and other changes of a cultural nature instituted, the result was greater pleasure and involvement in the learning process and increased academic success for the Native Hawaiian students (Au & Jordan as cited by Shade, Kelley, & Oberg, 1997, p. 58).

The above story (revealing stereotypes which could be similarly applied to many ethnic groups and gender-based assumptions) illustrates how examining one's own cultural biases and opinions is crucial. Being aware of children's cultural attitudes, styles, expectations, and values is key for designing helpful reward systems for their success. Following are some suggestions that may assist you in your reinforcement efforts.

Sample Reinforcement Strategies

Enjoy Your Students

First and foremost, enjoy your students and let them know this in as many ways as you can express it. Remember that your personal warmth and appreciation for each student is deeply received (Red Ribbons). Be interested in who they are, in what they already know, in what interests them, and in what and how they are learning. The greatest reward you can give children is the knowledge that you genuinely enjoy being in their presence.

Encourage Students for Many Merits

Be authentic and give specific praise only when merited, but look for the merits deserved by every child on every day. Distinguish between empty praise and constructive feedback and help your students understand what they have done well (Klassen, n.d.). Say, "You did a good job using persuasive language in your paragraph," for instance, versus saying, "That's good!"

Reward the Group

Recognize that many cultures value cooperation, collaboration, and unity above individualism, personal achievement, and competition.

You can reward the whole class or the learning group for their efforts and their good cooperation with treats, a good movie, or special day of play.

Learning as Its Own Reward

As much as possible, allow the love of learning, in itself, to be the reward for a student's efforts, in order to avoid developing a dependence upon exterior motivators, such as stickers, gumdrops, or even grades. Reinforce the value of what has just been learned or discovered by saying, "Isn't this a wonderful thing to know?" or "I'm just so excited that you have mastered this skill, because now you can ____," or "This is an amazing discovery you just came up with! Let's share it with the class."

Allow for Reward Sharing

When teaching in a school with a large Hispanic population, I discovered that most of my students wanted to share treats or rewards with others. A box of crayons as a winning prize, for instance, was quickly distributed, one crayon apiece, to other children in the class. I later realized how much other cultures also emphasize the value of sharing. When you do use exterior motivators, make individual rewards large enough or dividable enough for a child to apportion to everyone.

Talk to Parents

Honor a child's family connections by quietly telling the parents or grandparents, preferably within the child's hearing, what you appreciate about this student. Or contact your students' family members by e-mail, phone, or written message to share their child's successes.

Be Sensitive to "Singling Out"

Because some cultures do not place as high a value on individual achievement as they do on group cohesion, be sensitive to a child's response to being "singled out" for acknowledgment and adjust your approach accordingly.

Food for Thought

Because the matter of touching children was brought up in the above example of Hawaiian schools, I will "touch" upon it here. This is a sensitive subject in today's world, but worthy of deep consideration. Psychology tells us how important appropriate touch is to a child's healthy development, and most teachers know that touch is a method of feedback that many children readily respond to. It was exceptionally helpful for the Native Hawaiian students whose culture is very touch oriented. And yet there are more and more laws and rules that prohibit touching students, and just as many good reasons for this, for child abuse is real. Furthermore, sensitivity to cultural attitudes about touch is important. Hispanic and African American families are generally less averse to touching than those of northern European lineage, yet some African American children do not appreciate people touching their hair. In some Native American cultures, one should never touch anything that belongs to another without permission. Children of various religions are taught that the head is a very sacred part of the body and should not be touched by others. In some Asian cultures, touching another with the left hand is offensive. So it is difficult to offer a universal rule on the matter of touching, other than just being respectful, deeply aware, and sensitive without getting paranoid, which is always the wisest approach. Good culturally responsive teachers learn to navigate this complexity with openness, by fine-tuning their awareness of their students' comfort levels, sharing affection through touch with their students when it feels appropriate, always respecting cultural differences, and being willing to learn.

Good culturally responsive pedagogy embodies the meticulous ability to design your assessment and reinforcement methods in concert with your deepest intentions for equity and success. It is the willingness to step outside all norms to achieve your goals that draws you into the league of all the great teachers, known and unknown, who have come before you. When you *Catch Kids Being Smart*, when you *Expect the Best From Every Student*, when you apply *Multiple Modes of Assessment*, and when you create a *Positive Rewards System Attentive to Cultural Values*, you are weaving Blue Ribbons of powerful academic achievement into your pedagogical tapestry.

BLUE RIBBONS

QUESTIONS TO PONDER AND DISCUSS

- Did you ever have a teacher who believed you were capable of learning anything? If so, or if not, how did this affect your academic development?
- Have you ever observed the effects of the Pygmalion Effect on children? What was your experience?
- Do you believe that **Any Student Can Learn Anything**? If not, what are your beliefs or experiences that challenge this assumption?
- Are you willing to "try on" this assumption in your practice? What would be the value of doing so?
- What is the benefit to your student when you "catch her being smart"?
- Besides those listed in the book, what are two other situations in which you could *Catch Your Students Being Smart*?
- What is the difference between criticism and critique? Give three examples of both.
- What kinds of thinking skills other than a brain full of "right answers" do you want your students to carry with them when they leave you after a year? Do you, for instance, value originality, persistence, eagerness, or curiosity as much as you do the memorization of facts? List at least five more valuable thinking skills.
- In what ways can you acknowledge your students' developmental proficiency in the answers listed above?
- Do you have a tendency to want to blame the student, his family, or his environment when he is not meeting grade-level mastery? How can you reframe this belief (without raking yourself over the coals)? Try to erase the word "blame" from your vocabulary and begin thinking in terms of "cocreative responsibility."
- In what ways is testing a positive necessity? Do you see the value of looking critically at testing procedures? In what ways can testing be detrimental to growth and learning?
- In three or four sentences, how would you describe a healthy stance toward testing that a culturally responsive teacher should take?
- What kinds of rewards from your own cultural background have inspired your learning? Do you find these beneficial for your students? What factors might obstruct or hinder some students' learning with the use of these kinds of rewards?

(Continued)

(Continued)

- How many of the Sample Reinforcement Strategies do you already use? Which unfamiliar one would you like to add to your repertoire? How would you begin to apply this?
- At this time, which of the Blue Ribbons catch your eye and your enthusiasm for weaving into your teaching practice? How do you want to begin?

Purple Ribbons 7

Instructional Changes Are Made to Accommodate Differences

Whenever a teacher reaches out to an individual or small group to vary his or her teaching in order to create the best learning experience possible, that teacher is differentiating instruction.

—Carol Ann Tomlinson
The Differentiated Classroom

To teach all students well, a Culturally Responsive Teacher not only strives to address different instructional needs of the students but also endeavors to be aware of cultural and individual learning penchants and interests. There is so much research now available to help teachers accommodate instruction to meet differences in the pace, perception, interest, readiness, and cognitive aptitudes of our students, but it is not always easy to see how to integrate all this information in our day-to-day practice. It may seem like an insurmountable challenge to the busy teacher to become responsible for attending to the cultural differences as well. But in truth, these approaches overlap and serve each other. The CRT approach is most compatible with many current individualized or differentiated practices, so to the extent that you are employing these methods, you may already be accommodating cultural proclivities very well. We will consider various approaches to differentiation in this chapter.

But as a prelude to launching into these Purple Ribbons, I ask you to once again refer to the Stringing the Vertical Threads chapter to review another basic belief about teaching:

- **Comprehensive Learning Addresses the Head, the Hands, and the Heart**

What are your conscious or subconscious beliefs about this statement? Do you consider the whole child in your approach to teaching? Do you assume that preparing children to meet the real challenges of living includes more than academic success? Are you cognizant of the fact that academic achievement is exceptionally enhanced by addressing the doorways of all the senses (Shams & Seitz, 2008); by including movement, hands-on activities, rhythm, and muscular participation in the learning process (Jensen, 2008); and by conscientiously attending to the emotional/affective domain (Sousa, 2009)? Teachers who create an environment for thinking, doing, and feeling (head, hands, and heart) understand the symbiotic interplay of these various facets of being human. All children function and remember best when many aspects of their nature are tapped. So keep this Vertical Thread in the back of your mind as you proceed through the elements of the Purple Ribbons chapter, for the correlation here is fundamental to CRT.

In this chapter, instructional changes made to accommodate differences will be organized under three general sections: *Multiple Doorways to Learning, Cultural Norms and Styles,* and *Variety in Curriculum Design.*

MULTIPLE DOORWAYS TO LEARNING

The educational literature provides a broad range of ever-evolving learning theories to help us appreciate and address the diversity of individuals we meet in our classrooms, including personality inventories, brain research, and models for understanding the multiple intelligences of our students. In this chapter, we will condense much of this information into simple but cohesive and comprehensive formats that can serve your practice.

On the most elemental level, if, throughout the day, you simply think in terms of addressing the needs and attributes we have assigned to the right and left hemispheres of the brain, you would be expanding far beyond the traditional "one-size-fits-all" classroom that is often based on a predominant left-brain doorway to learning. Most publishers of textbook materials have updated their manuals to support whole-brain, differentiated teaching and learning strategies, but tradition and cultural bias for disproportionate focus on left-brain mentation still hold sway in many classrooms. This becomes most noticeable as students approach the higher grade levels.

We cannot clasp onto definitions of hemispheric function too tightly, for brain research tells us that the two sides of the brain are not so neatly divided. The left brain is not always "logical," for instance, nor is the right brain always "creative," and there are many factors influencing where and how information is processed and stored in the brain (Jensen, 2005). But our western understanding of intelligence has been almost exclusively oriented to the logical, analytic, linear way of thinking and perceiving. A general understanding of the differences of hemispheric function can help us see what has been missing from our teaching and how we can learn to become more expansive in our understanding of brainpower. By acknowledging the two generalized modalities of brain activity and intelligence, we can assimilate a more rounded view of students of all ages. To this end, the following dichotomies, if not taken too literally, can be a helpful conceptual tool:

Hemispheric Definitions of Intelligence	
Left-Brain	*Right-Brain*
Logic	Creativity
Analysis	Imagination
Sequencing	Whole Picture
Linear	Intuition
Mathematics	Arts
Language	Rhythm
Facts	Nonverbal
Thinking in Words	Visualization
Words of Songs	Tunes of Songs
Computation	Daydreaming

Both sides of the equation are valuable arenas for learning, and each category is an important aspect of our human experience. They are reciprocal and mutually enhancing, with the most effective learning involving both sides of our nature working synergistically. As our educational practice grows to match the findings of brain research, we can gradually retreat from prioritizing analytic, logical, and sequential ways of processing as the only measures of intelligence and begin to see how a balanced person and a balanced world need more holistic wisdom. This gives us further understanding and appreciation of the gifts that the children of many cultures bring to the American tapestry.

Takdir Alishabana, an elder Indonesian professor, was waxing eloquent. He loved engaging younger people in meaningful discussion. It was a warm Balinese morning. Shafts of sunlight filtered through the tropical trees at the small window, casting leafy shadows onto me and three American friends seated on the floor. Takdir, who was a writer and a teacher at the National University of Jakarta, was currently ensconced in his beloved Bali retreat center. Here he held symposiums for what was called the International Association for Art and the Future, connected with artists and visionary people from all over the world in creative conversation about the destiny of the Earth and her peoples. "The symbol of your Western culture is a line," he said to us. "It is linear. Yours is a Progressive culture: future oriented, accomplishment based, mental, and individualistic. Ours (Indonesian) is more Expressive. Its symbol is a circle: enmeshed in the traditions of the past, artistic, feeling oriented, and communal. As your culture and mine and others of the world meet and meld, the symbol of the future global culture will be a product of the two dichotomies: a line meets and marries a circle and becomes a spiral. The symbol of the future is a spiral, balancing thinking and feeling, stability, and progress. We will all be more healthy as a result."

"We can no longer afford to be half-witted," says Bernice McCarthy (personal communication, Lecture, Western Washington University, 1991), creator of the ingenious educational model entitled the 4-Mat System, a teaching approach that has addressed both brain hemispheres for over 20 years and is still widely used. Bernice's 4-Mat system acknowledges four kinds of learners (McCarthy, 1997). She combines her research into a simple, but comprehensive construct for describing and teaching to four ways that learners take in and process information. These are described in the box below:

4-Mat Types of Learners

Type 1 "Feelers"

These are the heart-oriented, innovators, group workers, morale builders, people-people who take information in by feeling and process it by watching.

Type 2 "Thinkers"

These students take in information with the intellect and process by watching. They are most suited for traditional educational practice. These are the analyzers and organizers, fascinated by concepts and learning best by reflection.

Type 3 "Sensors"

These learners take in information with the intellect and process by doing. They are typically the engineer types, those with spatial-bodily-kinesthetic proclivities and common sense. These are the decision makers, the doers.

Type 4 "Intuitors"

Here are the soloists, the high flyers, looking for adventure and hidden possibilities. They take in information by sensing and feeling and they process by doing. These Intuitors are the dramatic, friendly, stimulating energizers and visionaries in your classroom.

Food for Thought

The notion of Learning Styles has been a popular one for many years, and although it has a host of adherents still convinced of its exceptional workability in the classroom, a study by Paschler, McDaniel, Rohrer, and Bjork (2008) challenge the notion that teaching to the preferred "learning style" of a student brings the best results. They present the alternate viewpoint that students may have preferences in learning modalities, but there is questionable correlation between teaching to a child's assumed "learning style" and successful acquisition of the material. The study states that (1) students can absorb information just as well through approaches other than their "learning style," (2) it is the content, not the preferred "learning style," that should define the modality of the lesson, and (3) it might be detrimental to a student to cater only to his one supposed "learning style," rather than broaden his capacity for learning and retention through a variety of modalities. *What adherents of both sides of the argument do say, however, is that all learners benefit from presenting lessons and information in multiple ways that engage all the senses and both parts of the brain.* I believe that the Learning Styles theories began to liberate us from narrow pedagogical practices. The gifts, talents, and genius of learners who do not fit exclusively into McCarthy's type 2 "Thinker" learning mode have been and are still being ignored or dismissed in too many of today's classrooms, especially with the current overemphasis on standardized testing, where a lot of "grill and drill" is enforced. Approaches such as the 4-Mat program can speak to the preferred or most familiar doorways of learners yet also reinforce the material through portals not so familiar. Through such multifaceted approaches, we can stimulate greater retention and more balanced brain activity for everyone.

Brain research tells us that when information is delivered in a pleasurable manner through many sensory avenues, recall is "more accurate, more detailed, and longer lasting" and creative problem-solving abilities are highly improved (Medina, 2014, p. 171). The commitment to teach through *Multiple Doorways to Learning* is what is important here. Whether we are using a model of the bilateral brain, or one of eight kinds of intelligence, or one of four types of learners, all students benefit from encountering information in a variety of ways. We are each, to varying degrees, a combination of feeler, thinker, sensor, and intuitor, and interest is tapped and perpetuated, for everyone, through novelty and variety.

CULTURAL NORMS AND STYLES

There is an infinite variety of differences in the ways children are socialized into their particular cultural groups, and this socialization influences their cognitive styles. Before launching into a discussion of cultural prototypes, it is important to state some caveats. The discussion of generalized cultural tendencies can be both "essential" and "controversial" (Guild, 1994). Considering these generalities can certainly broaden our understanding of the diverse learning modalities of children from different cultures, but it is also *imperative* that we keep from locking into new assumptions that may not be true of individual cultures or of individual children. Prototypes can only take us so far in stepping away from old unexamined biases and assumptions before we as educators slip, perhaps unknowingly, into new ones. Discussing general proclivities of Asian or Asian American cultural styles, for instance, does not do justice to the exceedingly wide diversity of Asian cultures. Caution is also advised to avoid any assumption that certain proclivities belong to a child just because she comes from a certain cultural group. Furthermore, prudence is necessary to prevent seeing cultural differences as deficits for children. They are, more commonly, strengths. It is also essential to recognize that as peoples mix and mingle, more and more of our students are coming from bicultural, or multicultural backgrounds, giving us even more reasons to not pigeonhole them. It is important to remember that all cultures are richly diverse within themselves, that all children within a given culture are unique, and that intelligence within any cultural population shows up in a multiplicity of forms.

This is a delicate and essential balance to keep in mind, always making a genuine effort to truly *see* each of your students without prejudicial blinders and barriers. General knowledge about cultural *prototypes*, if not used as *stereotypes*, can be helpful for you as you broaden your practice into new dimensions of CRT. The following paragraphs provide a few examples of prototypical cultural styles in learning that may help you understand your students and fashion teaching strategies that connect with their strengths.

African American

Various studies emphasize how many African American children, because of the cultural milieu in which they are raised, tend to be very physically and socially active. In general, when learning and interacting, you might note African American children needing bodily movement, oral communication of ideas, and the aural development of natural sounds and rhythms (Guild, 1994). For many black students, their attentional style tends to lean toward extroversion. And like most children, they prefer materials that relate to their own environment and culture. Therefore, for them, CRT would include discussion, active projects, and collaborative work. They would need opportunities to move, to laugh, talk, and enjoy each other, with cultural music and materials interwoven into the curriculum.

Native American

There is a great diversity among Native American populations of which many teachers are often not aware. As of July 2015, there are 567 federally recognized tribes in the United States, and there is an enormous range of cultural variety among them. So it is most important, once again, to be cautious about stereotyping your students. Nevertheless, some generalities might be noticed. You may observe that some of your Native American students are socialized for growing interdependence, harmony with nature and all living things, and strong respect for the community, especially the elders. Their attentional style might tend toward introversion. Because these children are often traditionally taught to watch carefully in order to learn, their perceptual styles might relate well to remembering visual symbols and manipulating pictures and designs. CRT, for these students, would include quiet times for thinking and absorbing, much opportunity for observation with an emphasis on visual stimuli, many occasions for group interdependence, and numerous references to nature (Shade, Kelley, & Oberg, 1997). As with all kids, much of this depends upon how much the child has been socialized into a traditional cultural setting as opposed to a Westernized one.

Latino

In a similar manner, because community and family are extremely important in their cultural ethos, many Latino students are very peer oriented and place high value on relationship, on experiencing life to the fullest, and on the satisfactions of a group's success. Because of this, learning interdependently in groups is usually preferred to learning alone

(Griggs & Dunn, 1996). Being sensitive to the feelings of others is important, and many of these students will use jokes and humor to avoid verbal disagreement, since arguing is often considered rude and disrespectful. Latino students often express an extroverted attentional style, enjoying verbal interchange and play. Laughter and movement are beneficial doorways to their learning, as are opportunities to learn through talking and working together, including reciprocal teaching (Shade et al., 1997).

Asian and Asian American

Although there is an infinite variety of individual and cultural differences among the students of East Asian, South Asian, and Asian American families, a culturally responsive teacher might note that a receptive learning style, coupled with an attentional style of introversion, is the case for many of these students.

Family is of utmost importance, and older people are deeply respected. For such children, what the teacher announces is considered relevant and right and the student's role is to absorb, with little question, the mediated knowledge. Diligent repeated practice is emphasized for learning, rather than challenging discussions or arguments, which could easily be interpreted, on the part of the teacher, as rude or disrespectful (Mishra, 2012). Harmony, in many cases, is considered more important than "getting to the bottom of things." It is advisable to be sensitive to the fact that being "wrong" is seen as a disgrace or "loss of face" for many students from these and other ethnic backgrounds. So it is important to avoid putting children in spotlighted situations until they are more adjusted to, and relaxed with, the environment and expectations of your classroom.

Lanying was a second generation Chinese American student in third grade. Beth, her teacher, was an assertive, independent person, who believed very strongly in self-reliance and confidence. Beth assumed it was merely shyness that kept Lanying from answering questions directed to her or made her so reluctant to go to the board for a math exercise. Beth eventually grew impatient with Lanying's tendency to whisper, both to her and to her classmates. She wanted her student to "stand up and speak up for herself," and to "stop cowering." Lanying was, after all, a smart and capable girl, and her seeming lack of self-assurance began to rub Beth the wrong way. But overhearing Beth's remarks in the teacher's room, an ESL colleague invited Beth to join her for coffee one afternoon so she could share some information she had learned about Chinese cultural expectations. Fortunately, Beth was open to learning about these and found herself having much more understanding of the clash that Lanying was facing between the culture of her immigrant parents and that of school. Beth learned, for instance, that Chinese families often do not consider self-esteem to be as important as achievement; that they do not place much emphasis on critical thinking, questioning, or speaking up; and, to the contrary, have great respect for the teacher's authority in imparting unchallenged information. In these realizations, Beth found herself much less prone to annoyance with Lanying and discovered more gentle and gradual ways to help her express herself in class, thus respecting the values of her parents as well as assisting Lanying's adjustment to the expectations of American school culture.

Jewish

Jewish children, on the other hand, often learn to embrace challenge, debate, and confrontation guided by the tradition of "pilpul," which means to better understand something by questioning, challenging, and clarifying that which is presented. This is a cultural learning style that means no disrespect and traces back to biblical times, where Abraham even questions God to fully understand His relationship to humankind. Nurtured through the Talmudic and Idrashic literature, this tradition of dialogue, agreement, and disagreement is ingrained in Jewish culture and can often be interpreted as discourteous or resistant by the non-Jewish teacher who lacks an understanding of this cultural trait. In a similar manner, in order to show enthusiasm and interest to another and to offer one's "talk as a gift," the Jewish student may "overlap" in conversation (which can be perceived as interrupting by non-Jews), something that can be misinterpreted as a lack of attention or courtesy (Zucker & Taylor, 2004). Studying in pairs or groups is familiar to Jewish children in the tradition known as *havruta*, or "fellowship," which manifests as an extroverted attentional style. The belief that life is significantly enriched by the respect of others, that learning is deeply enhanced by two or three others' viewpoints, and that the individual profoundly needs society are inherent precepts of the broadly defined Jewish culture (Schultz, 2003).

European American

Children of European descent are extremely diverse, but awareness of prototypical patterns of cultural styles is also important here. As of this writing, the majority of teachers in the United States are of European descent, but often not fully aware of the culturally based assumptions they make and attitudes they carry about learning. As emphasized previously, it is essential for all teachers to become increasingly cognizant of the mindsets and expectations inherent in the cultural seas in which we swim. We do this in order to grow in our understanding of both ourselves and our relationships with all our students. Northern European American children are usually familiar with a focus on independence and individual achievement, competition, analysis, detecting, and solving problems, making comparisons and learning by doing. Personal confidence is a cultural value and they, particularly boys, are accustomed to asserting themselves against one another, if it seems warranted. These "westernized" children are often taught to treat others as equals and to deal head-on with problems. Looking another straight in the eye is considered a mark of honesty. (In other cultures, this can be considered disrespectful or an act of defiance, particularly if the other, such as the teacher, is considered to be of higher status.)

All of the above examples are admittedly cursory summaries of the kinds of attentional, cognitive, perceptual, expressive, and behavioral inclinations brought to you by your students from their various cultural backgrounds. These examples certainly don't begin to do comprehensive justice to any cultural groups, except to start opening your eyes to the width and depth of their diversity. Furthermore, even if you were to study another culture all your life, you would never be able to understand it fully. So don't be discouraged by your lack of knowledge. However, you can learn much that is important to know simply through humble openness and careful observation, remembering that one student's needs and expectations could be the exact opposite of another's, even if they are from the same cultural group. The main point for CRT is to allow yourself to be increasingly aware of your own cultural conditioning and to grow in your ability to capitalize on the personal and cultural strengths of your students. Since the responsibility to fairly address such diversity could be overwhelming at first, it is also wise to be gentle with yourself. Thoughtfully and incrementally introduce new behaviors and teaching strategies, being especially aware of the clashes in cultural expectations your students might be experiencing.

Related to the Purple Ribbons, differentiation is the key—approaching all learning objectives through a variety of modalities. Attentive to the social backgrounds of her students, a good culturally responsive teacher allows for balance between quiet work, individual work, cooperative work, debate, and certain levels of volume and activity, as we have discussed in the Yellow Ribbons chapter, knowing that children have different needs and tolerances for each style and tone of interaction. A CRT practitioner is respectful and responsive in her increasing awareness of her own and her students' cultural influences, open to noticing even the most subtle behaviors and proclivities, such as a child's comfort with eye contact and touching or his needs for personal space and distance from the teacher. And as I have emphasized in the Orange and Green Ribbons chapters, it is important to remember that all children benefit greatly from cultural music, arts, and culturally diverse materials utilized in the learning process.

Furthermore, the culturally responsive teacher is sensitive to, and appreciative of, the language diversity of her students, including the variety of dialects in which English is expressed by different groups. For example, as we have discussed in the Green Ribbons chapter, the lively, rhythmic, often witty, and metaphorical communicative styles demonstrated by African American preachers and singers and people in everyday interactions can be witnessed in the children who grow up in this rich cultural context and can be embraced by the astute culturally responsive teacher to facilitate learning for her students. From a CRT perspective, we certainly acknowledge that proficiency in mainstream English is a necessary skill for success in the world, and we must give our students much practice in oral and written formal academic English. However, it is equally important to value the multiplicity of informal and colloquial forms of expression that all language groups offer. Rather than seeing language differences as deficits, we know that rich variations in language can be complementary tools for living fully and creatively in a pluralistic society (Gay, 2010). We want to capitalize on this variety of expressive styles by allowing our students opportunities for diverse linguistic expressions in creative writing, drama, and daily conversation and to avoid making anyone feel deficient when speaking in their own language or dialect.

VARIETY IN CURRICULUM DESIGN

As a way of introducing our discussion about accommodating differences in your instruction, I want to focus on some of the insights I have gained from friends and mentors throughout my career. By doing so, I hope you might find inspiration in the pioneering work they have done and also avoid having to reinvent too many wheels. Moreover, I want to help you avoid that tendency, which is all too prevalent in educational circles, to jump from one latest theory or strategy to the next without in-depth appraisal of what are the most compatible and valuable methods for you and your students.

Bernice McCarthy has already been mentioned. Her 4-Mat System has been successfully adopted by countless school systems over many years. Because I have used the McCarthy model extensively, and have found it to be most effective in my CRT curriculum designs, I highly endorse it. It has been an invaluable perspective for helping me address the many differences that children bring to my classroom and for showing how I can incorporate a variety of methods to make learning rich, fun, and stimulating for both my students. . . and for me.

My former teaching colleague, Bruce Campbell, has added practical experience and application to Howard Gardner's Multiple Intelligence theories. His work is especially helpful to teachers concerned with meeting standardized testing requirements, while still maintaining lively, colorful, and interesting classrooms geared for teaching to diversity (Campbell, 1996).

In addition, individualized and differentiated instruction and layered curriculums, well developed by educators Carol Ann Tomlinson (2014) and Kathie Nunley (www.help4teachers.com), are essential aspects of Culturally Responsive Teaching. Their approaches are best described in their books, websites, and articles, and I encourage you to familiarize yourself with them. If you are utilizing any of these methods, you are, in fact, addressing the Purple Ribbons by accommodating your instruction to the learning differences of your students. My purpose here is to reinforce the importance of these approaches in curriculum design for CRT, to support your initiative in the teaching to diversity that you may already be employing, and to emphasize adding cultural sensitivity and awareness to the mix.

I promised you at the beginning of the book that the ideas offered would be simple and easily infused into your established curriculum. If you are, in fact, already thoroughly launched into a model for diverse approaches, simplicity will still be the case for you here as well. If individualized and differentiated instruction is new for you, however, then this chapter may seem a bit overwhelming. Proceed gradually with care for yourself!

Learning Stations are a wonderful way to diversify instruction. (Bruce Campbell served as a masterful model for me in this method.) Following is a description of how any identified learning objective for your grade level, in any subject, can be approached with the use of stations. Move into this creative and rewarding approach to instruction gradually and thoroughly, step-by-step, allowing what you observe about your students and their various needs, interests, and propensities to inspire and guide you. Cooperative Learning groups, as discussed in the Yellow Ribbons chapter, dovetail well with this model.

Learning Stations

To adopt the Learning Stations method, arrange your classroom into learning areas with tables, grouped desks, or gathered chairs. You may want to design them to address both "sides" of the brain, or the eight intelligences described by Howard Gardner (as I will demonstrate below), or you can design your stations to address Bernice McCarthy's four types of learners (which are in all of us!). Keep in mind that in addressing these differences in your students, you are not focused solely on one assumed "learning style" of each child, but you are giving each student numerous avenues to tap and develop his innate intelligence. And you are making the lesson engaging and memorable for all your students.

To introduce your students to this process, you can designate at least one lesson period of the week to Learning Stations. This new arrangement of your classroom and your schedule can take place over a series of weeks or months, adding one new station each week. More time can be devoted to this as you adjust to the increased movement in the classroom and your students get used to your expectations of them within the new structure. It is fun, when introducing Learning Stations, to make it a special-treat learning day, on Friday perhaps, after a week of focus on a particular skill. You can increase the amount of time you do Learning Stations as your students become familiar with the protocol and you find it worthwhile. Eventually, if you enjoy the benefits of Learning Stations, you could, as did my friend Bruce, use Learning Stations almost every day for the development of many skills.

The main "trick" for success in using this method is to take the entire class around to each of the stations at the beginning of each Learning Stations period, demonstrate what is to be accomplished in each of them, and to also emphasize the behavior expected at each station. As always, it is expedient to utilize cultural projects, music, stories, and games to address the basic skill being developed. Following is a hypothetical model of first-grade station-based differentiation, augmenting the math skills of counting and one-to-one correspondence. Assuming that the children have already had sufficient practice with counting and the correspondence between numerals and numbers, this would be a wonderful way to amplify and enhance their understanding. This design would work best with four to six learners at each station at any given time.

Sample Steps for Learning Stations

Story Introduction

To begin, read aloud to the whole class the Japanese story "New Year's Hats for the Statues" in *The Sea of Gold and Other Tales From Japan,* adapted by Yoshiko Uchida.

See PURPLE RIBBONS RESOURCES: Variety in Curriculum Design: Learning Stations.

Review Counting to 10

Review the week's lessons in counting by verbally counting to 10 in English. Then have the students count together with you as you point to the numerals on a counting chart or flash cards. Tell them that these numbers have different words but mean the same thing in many different languages. Verbally, teach the students how to count to 10 in Japanese:

(Continued)

ichi, ni, san, shi, go, roku, shichi, hachi, kyu, ju. You might want to have a Japanese counting chart for comparison, perhaps with Japanese numerals. (It would be fun and meaningful to have a Japanese-speaking parent or grandparent introduce these numbers to the students.)

Linguistic Station

Have the students dramatize the story, while you narrate it or use a recording. Have six cone-shaped Japanese-style paper hats (resembling those in the story) to place on the heads of five "statues" and that of the "old man." Have the children count the statues in English and in Japanese, then assign the hats to the statues. Do not worry about confusing the children with numbers in two languages. Young children have great capacity for bilingual learning. Allow them to walk like wobbling statues, chanting, "Where is the home of the kind old man, the man who covered our heads?"

Logical/Mathematics Station

Have worksheets with rows of differing numbers of Japanese hats and spaces for the corresponding (Arabic) numeral at the end of each row. Have students count the number of hats and write the numeral for that number. They can work individually or in pairs to do this. Have them color the hats creatively.

Musical Intelligence Station

Have the students watch a DVD or listen to a CD of Taiko drumming. Provide each student in the group with a small hand drum or rhythm instrument. (For less noise, provide circles of paper on a table to be used as "drums.") Choose one student as the first leader, playing a designated number of beats on the drum, with everyone counting as he does so. He then repeats that rhythm a few times. Rhythms between one and six beats are easiest for the followers to remember. The leader can decide upon the tempo, the volume, or the accent on different notes. All other students in the group repeat the first student's rhythm, together, for several rounds. Use a bell timer to give notice to change leaders, allowing each student in the group a turn to lead. (Be sure, with some prior demonstration and explanation, to make behavior expectations very clear in the beginning for this station, since drumming often stirs children's "juices" exponentially!)

Bodily/Kinesthetic Station

Have students work in pairs as moving "statues," taking turns at finding a set of 10 different body postures, one posture to go with each number (i.e., squat for one, stretch arms for two, bend for three, etc.). Have the students perform for each other, counting to 10 in English, and then doing so in Japanese. Note: You may want to save this station activity for a day when the drumming station is not an option, just to keep the noise level from being too overwhelming!

Spatial Intelligence Station

Create a hanging Japanese fish art project. Give each student a piece of paper with the outline of a *koi* (carp fish) on it. In the center of the table, have a large number of multicolored circles to be used as scales for the fish. Assign each student a numeral between 1 and 10, written on a piece of paper, and instruct her, when it is her turn, to hand out that amount of circles (scales) to each one of the others while they count together, beginning at 1 for each new child. Then allow the students to work quietly, gluing the scales on their fish outlines. They will have more than 10 scales on their koi, but some may want to count all the scales to show you how well they can count beyond 10.

Interpersonal Intelligence Station
(preferably a comfortable place like the Circle Corner)

Have the students sit in a circle with a pile of five large cards in the middle of the group, with numerals 2 to 6. Have the students take turns around the circle, taking the top card and discussing one thing they remember when they were that age. If they cannot retrieve a memory from a certain age, allow them to pick another card. But memories of birthdays are sometimes good for keeping track of the years. (The numeral 1 is not included here, for most students will not remember that age, and the numerals 8, 9, and 10 will not be here for the children have not reached those ages yet. The reasons for the absence of these numerals can be discussed in the group.)

Naturalist Intelligence Station

Have one or two books on Japanese flower arranging (Ikebana) available for the students to leaf through. Inform the children that the structure of Japanese flower arrangements is based on the number three, considered to represent heaven, earth, and human (or, in other descriptions: sun, moon, and earth). Provide empty aluminum cans for vases, flowers, twigs, and leaves. Allow the children to make their own Ikebana, using no more than three of each item for their arrangements, as is the customary requirement.

Intrapersonal Intelligence Station

For people from all continents and cultures, numbers often have meaning and value as aspects of life and the natural world around them. One, for instance, often represented the unity of all life, and was usually

(Continued)

(Continued)

represented by the sun, or a mandala. The numeral 4 symbolized the four directions, the four seasons, the four stages of life, and the four phases of a day. At the Intrapersonal Intelligence station read (or have an older student or aide read) the Numbers Poem to the students.

See PURPLE RIBBONS SUPPLEMENT: Numbers Poem.

Have the students illustrate the poem with paint or crayons, perhaps listening to soft Japanese music in the background.

Agendas

The amount of time needed to complete the assignments at each station always varies, so this is an excellent way for the teacher to incorporate another differentiation approach, called Agendas. Here the students have their own folders with personalized lists of tasks and worksheets that you want them to complete within the week, based on their needs and skill levels. If finished with one station before another is available, each student has a folder of activities on which to be working in order to stay on task.

Your Role

When your students are well accustomed to productive engagement at these stations, as mentioned in the discussion of Cooperative Groups in the Yellow Ribbons chapter, they become very independent learners and you are given the wonderful opportunity to step back and observe. It takes time to get to this point, however, so proceed in incremental steps. By building their group skills one or two stations at a time, teaching them the protocols by example and giving daily reminders as to the tasks and behavior expected at each station, you eventually afford yourself the freedom to either quietly observe and evaluate your students, or take individuals or groups aside for helpful instruction.

The above suggestions on Learning Stations, you will note, are all unified by the mathematics learning objectives of counting to 10, and one-to-one correspondence of the number values with the numerals 1 to 10. You have used the background theme of Japanese culture, although that is not your required objective, nor do you need to overemphasize it. In this way, cultural themes can be quietly woven into the context of your mathematics program, infused into the subtle backdrop of the learning process for all students, thus bringing the beautiful diversity of our world to life for them as they master the required skills at your grade level.

Hopefully, this Purple Ribbons chapter has inspired you to address the diverse instructional needs of your students in a variety of ways and to find even greater interest and fun in the teaching process itself. Your attention to *Multiple Doorways to Learning* and *Cultural Norms and Styles*, and your application of *Variety in Curriculum Design* will demonstrate a deep respect for your students and support and inspire them in the learning process. Because these kinds of lessons are so colorful, meaningful, and applicable when taught with multiple modalities in mind, you can be assured that you and your students will be meeting the required learning objectives with greater ease, grace, and enjoyment.

PURPLE RIBBONS

QUESTIONS TO PONDER AND DISCUSS

- Describe an example of a valuable learning experience you have had where the "Head, the Hands, and the Heart" were all involved.
- How would you have defined intelligence in the past?
- How has this definition been shaped for you by your culture?
- Are you open to broadening your definition? What statement could you make that would articulate a broader understanding of intelligence?
- Through what strategies has your own intelligence been best tapped and developed?
- What new arena of skill and information would you like to develop for yourself?
- Name three new "portals" that could serve you in developing this new arena? For instance, would you consider learning a new language utilizing rhythm and body movements? Or music? Or watching movies?
- Have you encountered behaviors in someone from another culture that either confused or irritated you? Can you look deeply into the possibility that the behavior produced a cultural clash for you? In what ways?
- Describe an experience you have had in another cultural setting, either abroad or within this country. *In general,* and without judgment, use a word or phrase to describe *your experience* of this culture's proclivities in the following:
  ○ What do you observe that they value in life?

(Continued)

(Continued)

- o How do they express it?
- o How is love expressed in this culture?
- o What have you noticed about their behavior patterns with children? With elders? Toward friends? Toward people on the street?
- o What senses do you think they utilize the most for understanding and experiencing the world?
- o In what ways did you feel different than the people in this culture? In what ways did you experience commonalities?
- What are the ways in which you have experienced differentiated learning? In what ways would you like to improve upon these methods in your own teaching?
- Take a typical learning objective for your particular grade level or the grade level you plan to teach. Briefly write down or discuss eight ways you could approach this subject through Learning Stations.

PURPLE RIBBONS RESOURCES

VARIETY IN CURRICULUM DESIGN

LEARNING STATIONS

- **Book**
  - *Sea of Gold and Other Tales From Japan*
    by Yoshiko Uchida, (1988) Creative Arts

- **DVD (Taiko Drumming)**
  - "One Earth Tour Special"
    (2004) Kodo

- **CD (Taiko Drumming)**
  - "Heartbeat Best of Kodo" and others
    (2006) Kodo Audio

- **Books**
  - *Keiko's Ikebana: A Contemporary Approach to the Traditional
    Japanese Art of Flower Arranging*
    by Keiko Kubo, (1962) Tuttle

  - *Ikebana: Asian Arts and Crafts for Creative Kids*
    by Shozo Sato, (2004) Simon & Schuster

  - *Ikebana: Japanese Flower Arranging for Today's Interior*
    by Michelle Cornell & Diane Norman, (2002) Rizzoli

PURPLE RIBBONS SUPPLEMENT
MATH POEM
(The Numbers Poem)

When at first we look at one,

We find it in the shining sun

For me and you

We count one, two

The day, the night,

The dark, the light,

The good, the bad

The gay, the sad,

The girl, the boy,

We count with joy.

They all are twos

That we can use.

Father, mother and child we see,

And count them quickly: one, two, three.

That we have four seasons we know very well,

As well as four elements with which we dwell,

Fire and Water, Earth and Air,

Are the four elements we share.

And four kingdoms of nature to you we can tell.

The number of fingers I have on one hand

Are one, two, three, four, five.

Five toes on each foot help me balance and stand.

Whoever counts all of his fingers knows

That he also has the same number of toes:

One, two, three, four, five, six, seven, eight, nine, and ten,

We count the hours of each day

And when we do we always say:

One, two, three—four, five, six—

Seven, eight, nine—ten, eleven, twelve.

We count the months in every year

And when we do, then you will hear:

One, two, three—four, five, six—

Seven, eight, nine—ten, eleven, twelve.

The different numbers of the earth

Have been around us since our birth;

But no matter how hard we try

We cannot count all the stars in the sky.

From *Math Lessons for Early Grades* by Dorothy Harrer (1985)
Reprinted with permission from Waldorf Publications (www.waldorfpublications.org)

Violet Ribbons   8

*The Classroom Is Managed With
Firm, Consistent, Loving Control*

> *Teachers who use these methods often find that the overall proportion of time dedicated to managing behavior is reduced. This means more instructional time becomes available. It also means that students (and teachers) have happier, more peaceful experiences of their school days.*
>
> —Amos Clifford
> *Center for Restorative Process*

In order for any of the other bright ribbons of Culturally Responsive Teaching to be effective, it is imperative to maintain the Violet Ribbons atmosphere of positive, respectful control throughout the day in the classroom. This could be said to be the heart of the work, for only within relaxed and focused classrooms can our students learn and thrive. As with everything else we have discussed, the classroom management skills of the teacher must arise out of deep awareness of her own cultural conditioning and growing understanding of the diverse backgrounds of her students.

Many teachers assume that all of their students share, or should share, the teacher's own beliefs about appropriate school behavior. From this unexamined assumption, they judge the child's culture or punish the child himself for being "unruly," or "disrespectful," or "unmotivated," when often the student has not yet learned what conduct his teacher and his school expect.

There are also teachers who, in attempting to be open to cultural differences and styles, make the mistake of not maintaining high expectations for deportment, attention, and on-task behavior from all students, and easily become frustrated and punitive when students get out of control. The Violet Ribbon of classroom management that speaks to firm, consistent, loving control is a delicate, but essential balance to maintain.

The Violet Ribbons touch upon a very sensitive but central issue in education when teachers of one cultural group are teaching students of another cultural group. The ways in which children are socialized to "behave," as mentioned earlier in the example of the Hawaiian children with non-Hawaiian teachers, can be very different from the socialization of the teacher and the ethos of the school. A culturally responsive teacher is careful not to make value judgments about certain behavioral proclivities, especially in terms of active, verbal, and enthusiastic behaviors versus quiet and low-key ones. But it is also essential for teachers to be very certain, first within our own minds, then with our students, about what deportment we expect within any learning activity.

Anna, my former neighbor and teacher in our city, felt that too many of her colleagues were resorting to "catching kids being bad," rather than using positive strategies and modeling behaviors conducive to learning. She said, "The problem with some of these teachers is that they are too enabling at first, then they crack down too hard!"

Becoming aware of your own unspoken standards is the first step. What kind of behavior do you expect for each activity? What is your expectation of controlled interaction? How much volume is appropriate for any activity? What kind of touching is suitable? How much movement is permissible in each case? This conscious review of your own expectations is necessary in determining which of your implicit standards you, as the teacher, want to preserve and which ones should be discarded, or used only for specific learning activities and not for others.

Allowing times for liveliness, social interaction, and a certain amount of noise, as we have discussed in other chapters, does not, in any way, imply disorderly or undisciplined student activity. On the contrary, equitable pedagogy acknowledges that learning success for all students requires clearly focused behavioral expectations on our part, and self-control on theirs. Our goal is to help our students grow from being dependent learners to independent learners who are able to motivate themselves and regulate their own behavior. We therefore have to set clear expectations and limits for them, always offering reasonable explanations for why we expect these. We adjust the amount of freedom we give them by closely observing what they can handle, and we allow increasing autonomy in their choices and activities. In all situations, it is good to give your students plenty of opportunities to practice appropriate behaviors before engaging in activities within a variety of school environments and pursuits: How do we behave in the classroom when we are involved in a lively activity? A quiet one? What is expected in the Circle Corner? How do we transition from one activity to another? From one station to another? How do we behave in various situations in the gym, on the playground, and in the cafeteria?

In some cases, you will be changing your expectations to be similar to the students' own cultural backgrounds, allowing for more noise and movement in situations, quiet conversation in others, or more thoughtful, contemplative silence in still others. Hopefully, as you discover many gifts the children bring from their cultures, you will begin to see (as we discussed with Culturally Inspired Teaching Strategies in the Green Ribbons chapter) that not only can it be good for our students that we incorporate new behavioral models but it can also be beneficial for us as teachers and for the learning process in general to adopt some new perspectives and practices.

It will not always be easy. There will be students who find you far too casual for their initial comfort, given the more formal expectations of the teachers and other authority figures from their backgrounds. Or there might be others who find your soft voice or assumed expectations so different from their home environments that they perceive you as weak and a good target for manipulation. Setting limits for behavior, honoring the dignity of each student, and allowing for the development of student autonomy is a delicate dance of trial and error (Steele & Cohn-Vargas, 2013).

The main thing is to be clear about what you expect; consistent and firm in reinforcing these expectations; engaging the whole class in determining the rules of conduct (which will be explained further); decidedly more educative than punitive; and, as far as possible, knowledgeable about the behavioral expectations within your students' cultural milieus.

You've got to have that "Mama voice!" an African American principal from Georgia said during a professional development session. He was speaking of the kind of approach needed for children of his own cultural group, referring to the strong, firm, no-nonsense voice that many African American children hear from their mothers. Of course, it would be a mistake to try to imitate cultural style, accent, or voice inflection if it is not authentic for you. Children are finely attuned to what is authentic and what is not. But the "tough love" firm approach, coupled with clear expectations, was the point of his message to teachers.

For teachers who prefer quietude and desk-sitting for their sense of control, allowing liveliness during different learning activities may seem like inviting chaos. However, it is good for us to stretch ourselves to realize that purposeful modulation between exuberant, expressive activities and those requiring calm, contemplative moods can be both educative and refreshing for our students. (As mentioned in the Orange and Green Ribbons chapters, your choices of cultural music can establish the right sound background to serve your behavior expectations.)

In my research and practice, I have discovered several practical strategies to establish a foundation for firm, consistent, loving control that can help us: *Invoking The Golden Rule, Establishing The Belly Button Club, Dealing Directly With Prejudice*, and *Applying Active Conflict Resolution*. For the remainder of this chapter, we will be addressing these strategies.

INVOKING THE GOLDEN RULE

The Golden Rule (also known as the Law of Reciprocity) is a beautiful example of a universal standard that people in most cultures perceive as an ideal (Robinson, 2015). Almost all children will have this tenet in their cultural foundations. Establishing this fundamental precept as a part of your classroom ethics sets the stage for conduct that is not merely externally motivated by knowledge of school rules and regulations but is also internally motivated, drawing upon the child's natural capacity for compassion. I have found that children have enormous aptitude for empathy, but it must be carefully engendered within the social setting so as not to be diverted by the all too often cruel "ways of the world." The wise teacher actively cultivates *The Golden Rule* in the classroom's ethical code, knowing that the ability to "put ourselves in another person's shoes" is fundamental to the growth of healthy individuals and a healthy society. Clarifying *The Golden Rule* as a class norm at the beginning of the year is an invaluable point of reference for classroom behavior throughout the year.

The Golden Rule

Golden Rule Books

See VIOLET RIBBONS RESOURCES: Golden Rule

Read aloud books about *The Golden Rule* and discuss its importance with the students. You may wish to introduce to your students the varieties of religions and philosophies that endorse *The Golden Rule.*

Class Motto

Create a sign as a class motto: "Treat Others as You Want to Be Treated." Hang this in an obvious place for constant visual reinforcement. Or you can hang a ready-made *The Golden Rule* poster.

Refer Back to The Golden Rule

When issues of conflict or disrespect arise, refer back to *The Golden Rule* and ask each student involved how he would like to be treated.

Many Stories/Many Discussions

Reinforce the understanding of *The Golden Rule* throughout the year with literature from a variety of cultures followed by class discussions.

A Variation on the Theme

With older students, it is fun to refer to the quote by George Bernard Shaw: "Do not do unto others as you would expect they should do unto you. Their tastes may not be the same." From this we can derive one of the many varieties of *The Golden Rule*: "Do unto others as they would have you do unto them (while still maintaining your own standards and self-respect)." This stimulates a good discussion about the fact that sometimes we have differing desires and needs regarding our treatment from others, but the bottom line is that we all want to be treated with respect.

THE BELLY BUTTON CLUB

I have found that when the students help to create the class rules, they have much more ownership of them and are more likely to feel the negative results of the infractions, learning very quickly to self-modulate their behaviors. Creating *The Belly Button Club* rules together is a most invitational approach to this.

Establishing The Belly Button Club Rules

The Belly Button Club Introduction

During the first few days of the school year, introduce the students to the idea that this class is *The Belly Button Club*, emphasizing that it is a club where everyone has the right button, everyone gets to belong, and nobody makes others feel excluded. Introduce "The Belly Button Song" for a class jingle.

See VIOLET RIBBONS RESOURCES: Belly Button Club.

(Continued)

(Continued)

Belly Button Club Rules

With a series of guided discussions, invite the students to help you create *The Belly Button Club's* rules of conduct. These should be thoughtfully designed, so allow time for discussion on these matters each day over a week or so. If you, or your school, have behavior management guidelines you want to introduce, you can present these first to establish a functioning relationship with your students from the first day. But let them know that these are general rules that you and they together will be modifying and strengthening by creating their own class rules in the next few days. Rather than using a series of "don'ts" in the statements, guide the students to state these in positive terms as those things that we "do." For instance, instead of saying, "Don't bother others with your arms or legs," write instead, "When we move around the room, we always allow others their space." You may find that they come up with many of the ones you want to incorporate, but made even better because you have helped them state these positively, yet in their own words.

Rules About Words That Hurt

Talk with the students about what kinds of words are hurtful and what kinds of words are kind. Guide them to include the rule that only kind, respectful words are appropriate, discussing the fact that put-downs and name-calling are never appropriate. Students who grow up hearing a lot of negative words in their households or neighborhoods will need a good deal of reinforcement and practice, of course. But giving them a safe place in which such words, expressed either toward them or toward others, are not allowed will give them a new model for relationship and greater awareness and practice for making better verbal choices in their lives.

Anti-Bullying Strategies

There are many good anti-bullying programs to implement in your school and classroom. In addition to many resources listed for NEA by Phil Nast (2015), the Welcoming Schools website (http://www.welcomingschools.org/) is an especially helpful resource for this purpose. Educate yourself and your students on the issue of bullying and always intervene to advocate for them. Create bully-free zones for your students within the classroom, on the playground, on the bus, in the cafeteria, or in any other school environment. It is good to emphasize this stand with the rule of "Our room (or school) is a Bully-Free Zone." Discuss the many forms of bullying, even the less physical ones such as exclusion from friendship and groups or starting and spreading rumors. Bullying is almost always related to the targeting of differences, whether related to appearance, culture, religion, language, food, race, gender, or sexual identity. It is important to recognize that all the work that you are doing to create a culture-safe classroom, helping kids to understand and value differences, is a major piece of your anti-bullying strategy.

Food for Thought

Hopefully, you have a schoolwide anti-bullying program. If not, I urge you to campaign for one. It is a serious national epidemic that needs to be consciously addressed and stopped before it has the opportunity to find a foothold in the life of your school. Teachers and administrators have a great deal of influence on children's behaviors, and this is a subject that needs to be on the top of our priority lists. Bullying must stop, for the sake of all your students. Because bullying is rarely done within the earshot of teachers and other school adults, it is important to be informed about the characteristic attitudes and tactics of bullying, to be a visible, vigilant advocate in the places where students interact, and to be hyperalert to indications that bullying is happening anywhere in the lives of your students. Counseling help or administrative support is essential for children who are not able to "kick" the bullying habit. Do not avoid or procrastinate in getting assistance when it is needed, for it is a very serious matter, with dire effects on your students' sense of worthiness, their school success or failure, and even their desire to live.

Positive Cultural Values

Emphasize values that come from the cultures of your students, such as Respect, Harmony, Friendliness, Effort, Humor, etc. Send home with each student a list of core values (you can choose an age-appropriate sampling from the list of core values in the Violet Ribbons Supplement).

See VIOLET RIBBONS SUPPLEMENT.

Ask the students to talk to their parents about which ones are most important to their family and their cultural community, circling five that each student considers the most important—ones that they do not feel they or their families could live without. (If English is the second language for some of your students, enlist the students' help, or get an

(Continued)

(Continued)

aide, to translate the list of words you choose before sending it home to the families.) When the lists are brought back to class, make cards for each core value that is selected, to be hung on the walls of the room. Reflect upon similarities and differences in these values. Suggest that your students add to *The Belly Button Club* rules the ones that you and the students recognize are most common to everyone.

Saying "Ouch!"

Teach the students how to respond to words that hurt by saying "Ouch!" This practice can diffuse tension by allowing any child to express hurt feelings without amplifying the issue, while allowing the one who spoke to be aware of the effects of their words, thus giving each person the opportunity to take greater responsibility for herself. This takes time and practice for anyone to master, but it is a tremendous social skill that all people everywhere would benefit by learning. Make this one of your ground rules: Whenever anything is said or done that hurts your feelings, simply say "Ouch!"

Belly Button Club Rules Poster

With your students, create an attractive poster displaying *The Belly Button Club* rules that the students have decided upon. Have all the children sign the document, then hang it in a noticeable place and review the rules from time to time, allowing the class to revise these and add more rules if and when the need arises.

Addressing Breaches of Conduct

Having good discussions about how you, as a class, stick to your rules and manage problematic behavior is a large part of your students' civic education. The main goal should not be focused on punishing wrong-doers (a practice education has inherited from the criminal justice system), but on teaching and learning behaviors that are safe, respectful, and conducive to learning. However you decide to approach the matter, consequences for not following the agreed-upon rules will need to be considered and agreed upon with another poster or a contract for them to sign. Lead the discussions with guiding questions, such as, "How shall we help each other remember these rules?" "What does a student need to do if she breaks a rule?" "How should other class members respond to someone breaking the rules?" In helping the class consider and create consequences for breaches in conduct, you will probably find that the students design outcomes that are far more punitive than necessary, so these will need to be modulated, of course, in accordance with the guidelines of the behavior management system you are using and your own sense of what is appropriate. I have found that following the protocols of Circle Time with a Talking Stick is a most profound way of addressing the more serious breaches, giving everyone a chance to express their feelings and opinions without rebuttal or blame, and then coming to a community decision about what is needed to go forward.

Restorative Justice and Restorative Practices are models and methodologies of harmonious interactions between people in groups: families, communities, educational environments, or corrective facilities. In talking circles, group members of the Restorative programs are invited to share their feelings, build relationships, and solve problems, and when offenses are committed, to help students address the wrongs and make things right (Riestenberg, 2012). Based, as they are, on improving, rather than punishing human behavior, these circles reflect the practices of Native American and many other indigenous groups all over the world. With the Restorative movements' use of Circle times and activities to serve both the individual and the community, you will find numerous similarities between these programs and the *Bright Ribbons* approach. I recommend that you and your colleagues research these Restorative Justice and Restorative Practice strategies and consider how they can augment your *Belly Button Club* rules and be adapted to the culture of your school (Maxwell & Williams, 2012).

Belly Button Club Practice

Have the students repeatedly practice together some of the rules before engaging in any new activities and in familiar activities that need behavior updates, such as how we move from one place to another, how we keep our arms and bodies to ourselves, what the quiet signal is, how we ask someone to move, how we share materials, what level of volume is appropriate in the various learning stations or during different activities, etc. One teacher had a noise thermometer on the wall to indicate what noise level was appropriate for any activity (Steele & Cohn-Vargas, 2013). As already said, much of what you expect may be implicit and not yet a part of a student's behavior repertoire. Never assume that your students are aware of your implicit expectations or that the student should "know better." You are always educating your students about the conduct you expect in all situations. Repeated rehearsal is an invaluable method for establishing your expectations of your students' behaviors in the classroom.

DEALING DIRECTLY WITH PREJUDICE

In my fifth-grade class in Washington State, I overheard one of my white students make the comment that the Swinomish (Native American people of the vicinity) were just "lazy Indians" with special "privileges" that took all the fish away from the white fishermen. I chose to address this comment immediately, especially for the sake of my Native American students, but also for the purpose of expanding the perspectives of all members of the class. For me, there was nothing on my teaching agenda that day that was more important than dealing with this hurtful comment. In that teachable moment, we called Circle Time to discuss the insensitive label of "lazy" and how each of us, including the boy who made the offending comment, would feel to be so considered. The students were very insightful, coming up with statements like "I think we just all want to be treated fairly." Later in the week, I arbitrarily divided the class into two groups and had each group research one side of the Native fishing rights issue, which has always been a major subject of contention in our state. Our class then had a debate with each "side" giving information from the perspective of its research. The next day, I surprised them by assigning each team to research and debate from the opposite viewpoint. In subsequent Circle Time conversations, it was obvious that the students were not only more informed but were also more empathetic about the needs and desires of all involved, on both sides of the issue. They learned how nontribal fishermen were frustrated by the growing number of rules, regulations, and fishing limits that they had to abide by, while observing their Native American counterparts not being restricted in the same ways, even on nontribal lands. The students also learned that the dwindling of the region's fish supply was caused, not by the Indians, but by Washington State's policy of issuing too many commercial fishing licenses and the development of canneries, combined with the construction of many dams in the area and the pollutions of industrialization. In addition, they discovered that the tribal governments were very proactive in developing and managing fish hatcheries for the state. Their research also provided more understanding of the perspectives of Native American communities, whose ancestors, in signing treaties giving up their lands, were guaranteed perpetual access to their traditional hunting and fishing grounds. In the end, one student's insensitive comment, and my decision to approach the issues in an educative rather than punitive way, led to an amazing level of growth for everyone in the classroom, including me.

While we can do much to build a safe and comfortable haven for our students, there are moments, as in the story above, when the ugly forces of bias, prejudice, and stereotyping enter your classroom and the lives of your students. It is most important that we are prepared to help our students navigate this painful arena of human experience. There are too many instances where unprepared teachers ignore hurtful comments and do not take advantage of teachable moments to dispel prejudice, wherein students are left feeling both judged and lacking the support of their teachers. We need to have the courage and willingness to take these issues on and to inform ourselves, right along with our students, of more facts and a larger picture. We want our students to become true leaders for equity in their schools, families, and communities. Everything that we have covered in this book serves this goal, but following are just a few more suggestions, some of which will echo the anti-bullying strategies you are presently using.

Suggested Ways to Reduce Prejudice

Begin With Sneetches

At the beginning of the school year, read Dr. Seuss' classic story about the Sneetches and have several Circle Time discussions about the pain of being labeled or excluded.

> See VIOLET RIBBONS SUPPLEMENT AND RESOURCES: Dealing Directly With Prejudice.

   Allow the children to volunteer examples of their own uncomfortable experiences with being labeled, or seeing someone else labeled or rejected, or even times they found themselves labeling another. Referring to the book, discuss the silliness of thinking that stars on bellies could make one group think they were better than another. Reinforce the basic premise of *The Belly Button Club*, a club where everyone gets to belong. Draw attention to how people sometimes think that making others feel excluded will make them feel good about themselves. Have the students suggest a myriad of ways that people can feel good about themselves and do reading or writing assignments on the subject. You will find the simple story of the Sneetches sets an excellent tone and can become a good reference point for dealing with hurtful behavior in the future.

Diversity Everywhere

Utilize the thematic collections you have developed from the Orange Ribbons chapters or posters that reflect the diversity of Nature (a field of diverse wildflowers, a garden, a bowl of multicolored fruit, a rainbow, a collection of seashells, etc.). Have frequent Circle Time conversations, art, or poetry assignments about how people are beautifully diverse, too, and how wonderful it is to live in a world created with so many diverse forms, colors, flavors, music, foods, cultures, and ways of being. Emphasize how everything and everyone has value and beauty.

(Continued)

(Continued)

Discussing the Harsh Realities of Prejudice

Children of all ages can learn and talk about the realities of cruelty, injustice, war, slavery, and genocide through age-specific children's books. Without bombarding them with an overload of negative information, and without making them feel guilty or responsible for the actions of their ancestors, you can still build their knowledge with facts, personal stories, and biographies of hardships. Part of our responsibility to our students is to teach them to be aware and informed about the problems of our world and to feel they can actually make a difference (Sapon-Shevin, 2010). They are, after all, the global citizens of the future. By allowing good time for such discussions, you help them deal with the inequities they hear and wonder about. But be sure to include information and conversation about the good and brave things humans do for each other as well.

Global Problems and Answers

For older students, pay attention to the national and international news topics and happenings that often reflect humanity's inability to deal positively with differences. Make a collection of news articles, asking the students to bring in their own examples. Ask them to bring in local stories and those from many countries. Divide these stories into two categories: (1) good things happening in the world and (2) problems happening in the world. In the case of the negative examples, ask the students why they think people behave this way. Then ask them what should be done: "What would you do if you were the president of that country? The owner of that big business? Or the mayor of that town? How would you teach people to deal better with differences?" You will find their answers are usually straightforward and simple—some worthy of being heard by our world leaders! Ask your students for suggestions, and together design actions that could help offer solutions to world events, such as writing a letter to a president or a newspaper, writing a song for peace, or creating a YouTube campaign among the children of the world.

Keep Reinforcing

Continue to periodically reinforce the worth and value of differences through videos and books created for this purpose and make time for following up with class discussions, writing assignments, or group projects. *Teaching Tolerance* is a wonderful website and magazine for free resources for kids at various age levels and strategies for teachers to minimize prejudice and hate (http://www.tolerance.org).

Avoid Spotlighting Children

Once again, be careful to allow students to volunteer their own information about themselves or their families, rather than putting the "Exhibit A" spotlight on anyone to "Tell us what it's like. . . (to be Russian, or Muslim, or any other ethnic identity)."

Inequities in Materials

As we discussed in the Orange Ribbons chapter, focusing on Inclusive Curriculum and Reading Materials, children's literature is increasingly inclusive of diversity, but there are still times when inequities are visible. These are teachable moments where such oversights can be made obvious to the students and their capacity for critical thinking can be stimulated through discussion. If you find yourself reading a story, for instance, that has any kind of stereotype, discrimination, or omission in it, be open about this with your students. For instance, you could ask, "I wonder why this book refers to Africans brought to plantations as 'workers' rather than slaves?" (This was true of a certain recently published history book!) "I wonder why there are no black or brown people in this book?" or, "What do you think about this sign in the picture that says 'No Girls Allowed'?" or "How are the families/neighborhoods/people in this story different from your own?"

APPLYING ACTIVE CONFLICT RESOLUTION

Even in a perfect world, we would still have conflicting viewpoints, for our differing perspectives do create friction from time to time, opening opportunities for us to expand our thinking and grow. But conflict need never be violent and can always be resolved, avoided, or at least lived with. Conflict holds learning opportunities within it for all involved. In my perfect world, conflict resolution would be considered a basic skill. Obviously it is not yet true, for our planet suffers from warring factions on all levels of human relationship, with cultural, religious, ethnic, economic, and gender differences being major catalysts for the drama. I believe conflict resolution is one of the most essential skills we can teach our students, and it can be introduced in a very uncomplicated, direct manner. When conflicts come up on the playground or in your classroom, it is exceedingly helpful to provide your students with a few positive steps to take toward the resolution of these differences.

In preparation for this work, teach the children a few of the following ground rules about conflicts. These could be incorporated into *The Belly Button Club* rules, or stand on their own.

Establishing Ground Rules for Conflict

I-Statements

Demonstrate, with examples, how to use "I-statements" that put the emphasis on one's own experience, rather than on the other person or people involved, such as "When she hit me, it really hurt, and I felt really sad," or "I'm so angry I want to scream!" as opposed to "She's a brat, and everybody hates her!" I-statements, with children and adults alike, serve to diffuse the temptation to put the whole blame on others, to insist upon one's own innocence, or to escalate the argument. "I-statements" also serve to access another person's compassion (or remorse!) much more quickly, because one's own feelings cannot be denied, and the need to protect oneself with counter-blaming is not aroused.

No Name-Calling, Ever!

Discuss the fact that name-calling, no matter how much one is hurting, is not acceptable. Teach them that "Even if someone has called *you* a name, take the high road. Don't participate. Say 'Ouch!' and move away or solicit help for upholding the class rules." (And repeatedly emphasize that seeking help to uphold the rules or protect oneself is never "squealing.")

Stick to Present Time

When dealing with conflict, teach your students to stick to the issues of the moment. Make no references to the past, such as "He's always doing that to everybody!" Teach them instead to use an I-statement in present time: "When he pushes me, it makes me really angry!"

Mock-Ups

For practice, describe to the students a hypothetical conflict that might arise on the playground or in class, and use two volunteers to demonstrate how it should be handled, with the steps for "Working It Out" below. Ask the children for examples of conflicts that come up in their lives at school and choose ones that seem appropriate for these practice runs. Do this several times at the beginning of the year to show the students what is expected. You will probably need to review the practice several times throughout the year. Once this procedure is established, you will find that children will experience great relief in using this method.

Steps for Working It Out

Everyone Cools Off

Allow the students to take a few deep breaths for a few moments before addressing the problem.

First Student Describes the Situation

Give one person a few minutes to describe to the teacher and to the other person involved (without interruption, using I-statements, and without name-calling) exactly what happened, from her own perspective. Be mindful to allow the students some time to describe the larger context, which is very important for many ethnic groups. What was going on before the conflict with this person? Be sure to give them a chance not only to describe the event but to express how it made them feel. No matter what is said, the other person must learn to listen and to wait until it is his turn to describe his side of the story. Giving each person a specific amount of time can help the students get to the point without feeling rushed.

Second Student Rephrases

The listening student paraphrases what he heard the other one say. At this point, he is not expressing his own feelings, just demonstrating that he was listening to the meaning of the first person's statements (Crowe, 2009).

Second Student Describes the Situation

Now the second person is given time to describe to the teacher and to the other person involved exactly what happened, from his own perspective (again, without interruption, using I-statements, and without name-calling). Once both sides have had a chance to express themselves completely, with I-statements, you will notice that the emotional charge has lessened considerably.

First Student Rephrases

The first student now has the opportunity to paraphrase what she heard the other one say, not expressing her own feelings, but demonstrating that she was truly listening.

Emphasize The Golden Rule and The Belly Button Club Rule

If applicable, emphasize *The Golden Rule* or the codes of *The Belly Button Club*.

(Continued)

(Continued)

The Next Step

Ask the participants to think about what might be the next step. If someone has broken a rule, what can he do to make amends or to restore good relationship? Affirm? Forgive? Thank? What can be done to make everyone feel better? You will often find them saying that they don't want to fight any more, or they want to shake hands and be friends, or they wish to be called by their own name, etc. If one student has hurt or offended another, give him the opportunity to come up with some kind of compensation. Allow the students a few moments to decide upon a mutual solution or compensatory action that is needed.

Or Go Around Again

If, however, after one round of these steps, the matter is not resolved, go around again, with each person describing what happened and how she felt about it. The emotional charge should be very defused by now. A final conversation could be tabled for the next day, but I have never found this to be necessary, for children usually just want to be seen and heard for who they are and how they feel, and this method gives the ample opportunity for just that. Furthermore, their attention span begins to wane as the emotions ebb, and you will sometimes find them laughing together if they think they might have to go over the matter yet one more time. Underneath all the agitation of conflict lies the basic human desire to be connected once again, which you will often observe in your students' mutual need for resolution.

Additional Considerations

Back to the Sneetches

If any child becomes the victim of a racial, religious, cultural, gender, or physically related slur or put-down, reinforce how painful it is to be judged for things like the color of one's skin, one's clothes, one's language, or one's abilities, etc. Remind the perpetrating student that it is against the rules of your classroom community to do so, dedicated as those rules are, to *The Golden Rule.* After she has had the opportunity to hear the effects her words have on the other person, have her decide upon something to do to genuinely make amends.

Private or Community Process?

You will need to discern whether or not any conflict is a moment to share with the whole class or just between the two arguing parties. Sometimes Circle Time needs to be called. But the conflict needs to be handled as soon as possible after it arises, so as not to let emotions fester, even if you must go into the hallway to talk. Students need to know that their teacher is aware of the social dynamics of the classroom and playground and will always intervene to protect them and help them deal with their conflicts (Steele & Cohn-Vargas, 2013). Sometimes this method works best with only the students involved in the conflict. But as the year progresses, with the children becoming familiar with the procedure and the class developing into a real community, it is often advisable to allow the rest of the class to participate in the conversation, sharing their own feelings (with a Talking Stick) and deriving the benefits of this learning experience. Everyone in the discussion needs to follow the protocol of using I-statements, staying clear of name-calling, and disallowing interruptions.

Mediators

Discussing painful situations with the entire class offers all students the benefit of learning to be mediators in this process and take an active role in intercessions for peace. Even when dealing privately with a matter in the hallway, a student uninvolved with the conflict might serve as a "mediator apprentice," coming with the teacher to arbitrate arguments, observing your success with interventions, and then gradually assuming responsibility to guide the arguing parties to resolution, following the steps for Working It Out. You will be surprised by how well students can handle the role of mediator, once they learn the techniques. They can begin to apply these practices on the playground, in the lunchroom, and any place where conflict arises, especially if a whole-school mediation training is endorsed. And what marvelous social skills they have gained by doing so!

Working It Out Poster

Create a class poster entitled "Working It Out," with the steps discussed above simplified for your students, as illustrated below:

Working It Out

We take turns telling exactly what happened.
We listen to each other with no interruption.
We include our feelings.

(Continued)

(Continued)

> We avoid name-calling.
> We only make I-statements.
> We talk about this one incident only.
> We rephrase what the other person has said in our own words.
> What Belly Button Club Rule do we need to remember?
> What do we want to do for the next step?
> Can we agree on the next step?
> We can go around again if we need to.

By invoking *The Golden Rule*, establishing *The Belly Button Club*, *Dealing Directly With Prejudice*, and teaching your students how to engage in *Active Conflict Resolution*, you will come to realize how much the Violet Ribbons provide the structural framework children need to feel safe and strong in their environment. With these measures in place, they know exactly what is expected, they have had a hand in designing these expectations, and they know what the results of their behavior choices will be. They learn to be deliberate and intentional about overcoming injustices, and they increasingly develop the skills to deal with conflicts and disagreements. Although the social skills of these Violet Ribbons may not yet be considered "basic skills," and they do not show up on standardized tests, they are *very basic* to human existence. They are skills that too many adults in this world, heretofore, have not mastered. By taking on the responsibility of deliberately teaching these life skills, you are giving both your students and the world a rare gift.

VIOLET RIBBONS

QUESTIONS TO PONDER AND DISCUSS

- Imagine one snapshot moment in your ideal, relaxed, and focused classroom. What are your students doing? How are they behaving? From this snapshot, what can you say is your comfort zone for optimum student behavior?
- Have you ever been in a setting (in school or elsewhere) where others' cultural behavior is not within your comfort zone? What was your reaction?
- If you were a visiting student in a foreign culture, what would you want from your teacher in order to learn the expected protocols?
- List the characteristics of a good behavior that you would expect of your students in the following kinds of activities (include voice volume, the kind of movement allowed, and ways to show respect for others):
  o pair and share conversation with a partner
  o dancing to lively music
  o Circle Time discussion
  o getting ready to go to lunch
  o moving from one station to another
  o coming in from recess
  o friendly debate in a cooperative learning group
  o listening to you, the teacher, describe a lesson
- Have you ever considered the social importance of invoking *The Golden Rule* with your students? What does it mean to you? Is it basic to your understanding of human ethics?
- Name five benefits you think might be derived by establishing *The Belly Button Club* in your classroom.
- How committed do you feel to eradicating bullying in your classroom and school? Do you feel that it is part of your job? If not, whose job is it?
- Where have you felt the effects of bias and prejudice in your relationships? How did you feel? What actions did you take or not take? What do you wish had been done to help you or others navigate the situation?
- What skills do you think you need to learn to deal with students' prejudiced or judgmental behaviors?
- How do you deal with conflicts in your personal life? Do you avoid them? Do you find yourself reacting vehemently? Do you wish you

(Continued)

(Continued)

weren't so "wishy-washy"? Have you learned any specific tools for *Applying Active Conflict Resolution*?

- How does your personal experience with conflict affect your ability to deal with the conflicts of your students? Do you already have an established and helpful method?
- Describe how you want to improve your skills in firm, consistent, loving control of your classroom.

VIOLET RIBBONS RESOURCES

(All resources available at Amazon.com unless otherwise indicated.)

INVOKING THE GOLDEN RULE

- **Books**
  - *Adventures at Walnut Grove*
    by Dana Lehman & Judy Lehman (illus.), (2007) Lehman
  - *Do Unto Otters*
    by Laurie Keller, (2008) Bank Street
  - *The Golden Rule*
    by Ilene Cooper & Gabi Swiatkowska (illus.), (2007) Abrams
  - *The Golden Rule (Idea Reader Series)*
    by Caryn Sonberg, (2005) Ballard & Tighe
  - *Confucius: The Golden Rule*
    by Russell Friedman (author) & Frederic Clement (illus.), (2002)
    Arthur A. Levine
  - *Yoon and the Jade Bracelet*
    by Helen Recorvits & Gabi Swiatkowska (illus.), (2008) Farrar,
    Straus, & Giroux
- **Posters**
  - The Golden Rule
    by Norman Rockwell, Google: Golden Rules Poster for Classroom
  - The Golden Rule (other versions)
    Google: Golden Rules Poster for Classroom

THE BELLY BUTTON CLUB

- **Song**
  - "The Belly Button Song" Music for Aardvarks and Other Mammals
    by David Weinstone, (2004) Putumayo Kids Presents: Sing Along
    With Putumayo MP3 Download
- **Books**
  - *Auggie and Me: Three Wonder Stories*
    by R. J. Palacio, (2015) Alfred A. Knopf

o *Cliques, Phonies, and Other Baloney*
by Trevor Romain, (1998) Free Spirit

o *Diary of a Minecraft Zombie*
by Herobrine Books, (2015) Herobrine

o *I'm No Bully, Am I?*
by Felicia Williams, (2012) Xlibris

o *Just Kidding*
by Trudy Ludwig & Adam Gustavson, (2006) Tricycle

o *My Secret Bully*
by Tracy Ludwig and Abigail Marble, (2004) Riverwood

o *The Recess Queen*
by Alexis O'Neill & Laura Huliska-Beith, (2002) Scholastic

o *Sorry!*
by Trudy Ludwig & Maurie Manning, (2006) Tricycle

o *Spaghetti in a Hotdog Bun*
by Maria Dismondy & Kimberly Shaw-Peterson (illus.), (2008) Bookbaby

o *Stand Tall, Molly Lou Melon*
by Patty Lovall & David Catrow, (2001) G.P. Putman

o *Stick and Stone*
by Beth Ferry & Tom Lichenheld (illus.), (2015) HMH

DEALING DIRECTLY WITH PREJUDICE

- **Books**
  o *Sneetches and Other Stories*
  by Dr. Seuss, (1961) Random House

  o *All the Colors of the Earth*
  by Sheila Hamanaka, (1994) HarperCollins

  o *Almond Cookies and Dragonwell Tea*
  by Cynthia Chin Lee & You-Shan Tanh (illus.), (1993) Polychrome Pub. Corp.

  o *Brown Girl Dreaming*
  by Jacqueline Woodson, (2014) Penguin

o *The Christmas Menorahs: How a Town Fought Hate*
   by Janice Cohn & Bill Farnsworth (illus.),

o *Friends From the Other Side*
   by Gloria E. Anzaldua & Consuelo Méndez (illus.), (1997) Children's Book Press

o *Heart and Soul: The Story of America and African Americans*
   by Kadir Nelson, (2013) HarperCollins

o *How Tia Lola Came to Stay*
   by Julia Alvarez, (2001) Yearling

o *A Life Like Mine*
   by UNICEF & Harry Belafonte, (2005) DK Children & UNICEF

o *Mixed Me*
   by Taye Diggs & Shane W. Evans (illus.), (2015) Feiwel & Friends

o *One Crazy Summer*
   by Rita Williams-Garcia, (2010) HarperCollins

o *P.S. Be Eleven*
   by Rita Williams-Garcia, (2013) HarperCollins

o *Painted Words, Spoken Memories*
   by Aliki, (1998) Greenwillow

o *Ruby's Wish*
   by Shirin Yim & Sophie Blackall (illus.), (2002) Chronical

o *Stella by Starlight*
   by Sarah Jane Coleman, (2015) Atheneum

o *The Story of Ruby Bridges*
   by Robert Coles & George Ford (illus.), (1995) Scholastic

o *Terrible Things: An Allegory of the Holocaust*
   by Eve Bunting & Steve Gammel (illus.), (1989) Jewish Publication Society

o *The Unbreakable Code*
   by Sara Hoagland Hunter & Julia Miner (illus.), (2007) Publishers Weekly

See excellent age-appropriate Bibliography of Children's Books from Understanding Prejudice Reading Room under the following topics:

o Multicultural and Cross-Cultural Perspectives
o Talking About Color and Diversity
o Slavery and Resistance
o Harriet Tubman and the Underground Railroad
o Jim Crow, Segregation, and Integration
o The Civil Rights Movement
o The Story of Rosa Parks; Martin Luther King, Jr.
o Interracial Families and Friendships Thanksgiving and Native People of the Americas
o Immigration and Language
o The Internment of Japanese Americans
o Anti-Semitism and the Holocaust
o Holidays and Religious Diversity
o Women's Equality and Equal Rights
o Challenging Gender Norms
o Families With Lesbian or Gay Members
o Physical Disabilities and Differences
o Learning Disabilities and Cognitive Special Needs
o Dealing With the Stigma of HIV/AIDS
o Other Forms of Stigmas

(http://www.understandingprejudice.org/readroom/kidsbib.htm)

VIOLET RIBBONS SUPPLEMENT
LIST OF POSITIVE CORE VALUES

Accountability	Efficiency	Innovation	Recognition
Accuracy	Emotional Health	Inspiring Others	Relaxation
Achievement	Empowerment	Integrity	Reliability
Adventurous	Encouragement	Joy	Respect
Ambitious	Environment	Justice	Respected
Appreciative	Equality	Love of Learning	Respectful
Artistic	Excellence	Loving	Responsibility
Athletic	Excitement	Loyalty	Risk-Taking
Balance	Faithfulness	Mental Health	Safety
Beauty	Family	Mentoring	Security
Belonging	Fitness	Motivation	Self-Expression
Career	Flexibility	Nurturing	Sensitivity
Caution	Forgiveness	Obedience	Service
Collaboration	Freedom	Open-Mindedness	Silence
Commitment	Frugality	Optimism	Simplicity
Communication	Fun	Orderliness	Sincerity
Community	Generosity	Passion	Solitude
Compassion	Gentleness	Patience	Stability
Competence	Genuineness	Peace	Success
Competition	Good Taste	Perfection	Teaching
Consistency	Growth	Performance	Teamwork
Courage	Hard Work	Persistence	Tolerance
Creativity	Harmony	Physical Health	Tranquility
Curiosity	Honesty	Positivity	Transparency
Dedication	Humility	Productivity	Trust
Dependability	Humor	Profit	Vision
Determination	Impacting People	Protect/Care for Children	Wisdom
Diligence	Independence	Protect/Care for Elderly	
Discipline/Order	Individuality	Purity	
Diversity	Influence	Quality	

©iStockphoto.com/Jani Bryson

Conclusion

By now you can see how deeply Culturally Responsive Teaching reaches into the heart of everything you do in the classroom. Hopefully, you will never perceive CRT as an "add-on" or a "have-to," but a deep commitment to a creative and compassionate way of teaching that has taken hold of you and permeates every fiber of your vocation. As I have tried to demonstrate, CRT is not about following strict, step-by-step procedures outlined for you by textbook companies. It is about appreciating your own professional ingenuity, resourcefulness, and knowledge of your students. It is about adopting CRT guidelines in a way that is kind and considerate to yourself and empowering to your students, yet always acknowledging the need for further growth toward greater competency in this kind of pedagogy.

Many artists rarely feel finished with their compositions but continue to add and rearrange their work until some trusted friend tells them it's finally time to stop! However, Culturally Responsive Teaching is a masterpiece that is ongoing—an infinite process—and there is a certain joy in knowing that you are never going to get it done. For the creative teacher, every day offers new inspirations to weave more bright ribbons into her lessons, and that is how we remain passionate about our work.

Culturally Responsive Teaching is truly an art, as the original Greek meaning of art, *harmos*—"a row of threads in a loom"—implies. It is the art of allowing ourselves to become more whole and fulfilled in our teaching roles. It is the art of truly serving the amazing variety of our students, with deep respect for their cultures and their personhood. And, in the end, it is about creating a more harmonious society in which diversity is valued for the rich stimulation, growth, and enjoyment of life that it offers, and in which learning is meaningful, delightful, successful, and empowering. I wish you well as you further develop your own unique, rich, intricately interwoven tapestry of this beautiful teaching art!

References

Aaronson, J., & Steele, C. (2005). Stereotypes & the fragility of academic competence, motivation, and self-concept. In A. Elliot & C. Dwek (Eds.), *Handbook of competence & motivation* (pp. 436–456). New York, NY: Guilford.

Appiah, K. (2007). *Cosmopolitanism: Ethics in a world of strangers.* New York, NY: W. W. Norton.

Banks, J. (2008). *An introduction to multicultural education.* Boston, MA: Pearson Education.

Bates, S. (n.d.a). *The real story of Thanksgiving.* Manataka American Indian Council. Retrieved July 17, 2015, from www.manataka.org/page 269.html

Bates, S. (n.d.b). *The truth about Thanksgiving.* [Video File]. Retrieved July 17, 2015, from https://www.youtube.com/watch?v=IP-APn__JT0

Blankstein, A., & Noguera, P. (Eds.) (2015). *Excellence through equity: Five principles of courageous leadership to guide achievement.* Thousand Oaks, CA: Corwin.

Bryson, B. (1990). *The mother tongue: English and how it got that way.* New York, NY: William Morrow.

Campbell, B. (1996). Multiple intelligences in the classroom. *Context Institute.* Retrieved from http://www.context.org/iclib/ic27/campbell/

Chamberlain, S. P. (2004, November). An interview with Asa G. Hilliard, III and Alba Ortiz on the effects of the "no child left behind act" on diverse learners. [PDF file]. *SAGE Journals Vol 40, #2.*

Chenowith, K. (2007). *It's being done: Academic success in unexpected schools.* Cambridge, MA: Harvard Education.

Clark, R. (2003). *The essential 55.* New York, NY: Hyperion.

Clifford, A. (n.d.). *Teaching restorative practices with classroom circles.* [PDF file]. Retrieved February 11, 2016, from http://www.healthiersf.org/RestorativePractices/Resources/documents/RP Curriculum and Scripts and PowePoints/Classroom Curriculum/Teaching Restorative Practices in the Classroom 7 lesson Curriculum.pdf

Cohen, E. (2014). *Designing groupwork: Strategies for the heterogeneous classroom.* New York, NY: Teachers College Press.

Colorado, C. (2007). Cooperative Learning Strategies. In *Colorin Colorado: Helping children read. . . and succeed.* Retrieved August 4, 2015, from http://www.colorincolorado.org/educators/content/cooperative/

Crowe, C. (2009, February). Coaching children in handling everyday conflicts. *Responsive Classroom Newsletter.* Retrieved from https://www.responsiveclassroom.org/article/coaching-children-handling-everyday-conflicts

Dixon, A. (2011). Kindness makes you happy and happiness makes you kind. Retrieved from http://greatergood.berkeley.edu/article/item/kindness_makes_you_happy_and_happiness_makes_you_kind

Dove, M., & Honigsfeld, A. (2013). *Common core for the not-so-common learner: English language arts strategies grades k–5*. Thousand Oaks, CA: Corwin.

Fairman, E. (2010). *A steiner-waldorf mathematics resource: Grades 1–8*. Chatham NY: Waldorf.

Fredericks, L. (1997). Developing literacy skills through storytelling. *The Resource Connection*. Retrieved from https://www.ecu.edu/cs-lib/trc/upload/Developing-Literacy-Skills-Through-Storytelling-2.pdf

Gardner, H. (2009). Big thinkers: Howard Gardner on multiple intelligences. [Video file]. *Edutopia*. Retrieved October 12, 2016, from http://www.edutopia.org/multiple-intelligences-howard-gardner

Gardner, H. (2011). Frames of mind: The theory of multiple intelligences. New York, NY: Basic Books.

Gay, G. (2003). *Becoming multicultural educators: Personal journey toward professional agency*. San Francisco, CA: Jossie-Bass.

Gay, G. (2006). Connections between classroom management and culturally responsive teaching. In C. M. Evertson & C. S. Weinstein (Eds.), *Handbook of classroom management: Research, practice, and contemporary issues* (pp. 343–370). Mahwah, NJ: Erlbaum.

Gay, G. (2010). *Culturally responsive teaching: Theory, research & practice*. New York, NY: Teachers College Press.

Gay, G., & Kirkland, K. (2003). Developing cultural critical consciousness and self-reflection in preservice teacher education. *Theory Into Practice, vol. 42*, College of Education, Ohio State University. Retrieved February 2016 from http://citeseerx.ist.psu.edu/viewdoc/download?doi=10.1.1.460.7961&rep=rep1&type=pdf

Gillard, M. (1996). *Storyteller, story teacher: Discovering the power of storytelling for teaching and living*. York, MA: Stenhouse.

Gillies, R. (2007). *Cooperative learning: Integrating theory and practice*. Thousand Oaks, CA: Sage.

Ginsberg, M. (2011). *Transformative professional learning: A system to enhance teacher and student motivation*. Thousand Oaks, CA: Corwin.

GLAD (Guided Language Acquisition Design). Retrieved from http://begladtraining.com/

Glossary of Education Reform (2015). *Hidden Curriculum*. Retrieved from http://edglossary.org/hidden-curriculum/

Gonzalez, N., Greenberg, J., & Velez, C. (2001). *Funds of knowledge: A look at Luis Moll's research into hidden family resources*. [PDF file]. Retrieved from http://edsource.org/wpcontent/uploads/Luis_Moll_Hidden_Family_Resources.pdf

Griggs, S., & Dunn, R. (1996). Hispanic-American students and learning style. *Eric Digest*. Retrieved from http://www.ericdigests.org/1996-4/hispanic.htm

Guild, P. (1994). The culture/learning style connection. *Educational Leadership*. Retrieved from http://www.ascd.org/publications/educational-leadership/may94/vol51/num08/The-Culture~Learning-Style-Connection.aspx

Hammond, Z. (2015). *Culturally responsive teaching and the brain: Promoting authentic engagement and rigor among culturally and linguistically diverse students*. Thousand Oaks, CA: Corwin.

Harrer, D. (2007). *Math lessons for early grades*. Chatham, NY: Waldorf Publications.

Hattie, J. (2009). *Visible learning: A synthesis of over 800 meta-analyses relating to achievement.* Thousand Oaks, CA: Corwin.

Hattie, J. (2012). *Visible learning for teachers.* New York, NY: Routledge.

Hilliard, A. (2004). *Assessment equity in a multicultural society.* Retrieved from http://education.jhu.edu/PD/newhorizons/strategies/topics/Assessment Alternatives/hilliard.htm

Howard, G. (2015). *We can't lead where we won't go: An educator's guide to equity.* Thousand Oaks, CA: Corwin.

Hughes-Hassell, S., Barkley, H., & Hoehler, E. (2009). Promoting equity in children's literacy instruction: Using a critical race theory framework to examine transitional books. *School Library Media Research, 12,* 1–20.

Jensen, E. (2005). *Teaching with the brain in mind.* Alexandria, VA: Association for Supervision and Curriculum Development.

Jensen, E. (2008). *Brain based learning: The new paradigm of teaching.* Thousand Oaks, CA: Corwin.

Johnson, R., & Johnson. D. (2009). *Circles of learning: Cooperation in the classroom.* Edina, MN: Interaction.

Johnson, R., Johnson. D., & Halubec, E. (2007). *The nuts and bolts of cooperative learning.* Edina, MN: Interaction.

Kennedy-White, K., Zion, S., Kozleski, E., & Fulton, M. (2005). Cultural identity and teaching. *On Point Series.*

Klassen E. (n.d.). Encouragement or praise for children? *iCHED.* Retrieved 2015 from http://www.iched.org/cms/scripts/page.php?item_id=encouragement_praise&highlight=klassen

Lindquist, T., & Selwyn, D. (2000). *Social studies at the center: Integrating kids, content, and literacy.* Portsmouth, NH: Heinemann.

Marzano, R. (2007). *The art and science of teaching.* Alexandria, VA: ASCD.

Marzano, R., Pickering, D., & Pollock, J. (2001). *Classroom instruction that works: Research based strategies for increasing student achievement.* Alexandria, VA: ASCD.

Maxwell, J., & Williams, M. (2012). *Safe & peaceful schools: Addressing conflict & eliminating violence.* Thousand Oaks, CA: Corwin.

McCarthy, B. (1997). A tale of four learners: 4Mat's learning styles. *Educational Leadership.* Retrieved from http://www.ascd.org/publications/educational-leadership/mar97/vol54/num06/A-Tale-of-Four-Learners@-4MAT's-Learning-Styles.aspx

Medina, J. (2014). *Brain rules: Twelve principles for surviving and thriving at work, home and school.* Seattle, WA: Pear Press.

Mishra, S. (2012). Asian learning & teaching styles: Tradition & modernity. In E. Christopher (Ed.), *Communication across cultures.* Bassingstoke, HPH, United Kingdom: Palgrave Macmillan.

Moll, L. (2014, October 17). *Funds of knowledge.* [Video file]. Retrieved from https://www.youtube.com/watch?v=okyqK-KGJI0

Nast, P. (2015). Teaching students to prevent bullying: Curriculum resources address identifying, confronting and stopping bullying. Retrieved from http://www.nea.org/tools/lessons/teaching-students-to-prevent-bullying.html

Nieto, S., & Bode, P. (2013). School reform and student learning: A multicultural perspective. In J. Banks & C. Banks (Eds.), *Multicultural education: Issues & perspectives.* Hoboken, NJ: John Wiley & Sons.

Norfolk, S., Stenson, J., & Williams, D. (2006). *The storytelling classroom: Applications across the curriculum.* Westport, CT: Libraries Unlimited.

Orlich, D., Harder, R., Callahan, R., Trevisan, M., Brown, A., & Miller, D. (2013). *Teaching strategies: A guide to effective education.* Belmont, CA: Wadsworth Cengage Learning.

Palmer, P. (1993). *To know as we are known: Education as a spiritual journey.* New York, NY: HarperCollins.

Paschler, H., McDaniel, M., Rohrer, D., & Bjork, R. (2008). Learning styles: Concepts & evidence [PDF file]. *Psychological Science in the Public Interest,* *9*(3). Retrieved from https://www.psychologicalscience.org/journals/pspi/PSPI_9_3

Ravitch, D. (2011). *The death & life of the great American school system: How testing & choice are undermining education.* New York, NY: Basic Books.

Riestenberg, N. (2012). *Circle in the square: Building community and repairing harm in school.* St. Paul, MN: Living Justice Press.

Robinson, B. (2015). The "golden rule": Passages from various religious texts. *Religious Tolerance,.* Retrieved from http://www.religioustolerance.org/reciproc2.htm

Rosenthal, R., & Jacobson, L. (2003). *Pygmalion in the classroom: Teacher expectation & pupils' intellectual development.* Norwalk, CT: Crown House.

Rutherford Institute. (2015). *The twelve rules of Christmas.* Retrieved from https://www.rutherford.org/publications_resources/legal_features/the_twelve_rules_of_christmas2

Saifer, S., Edwards, K., Ellis, D., Ko, L., & Stuczynski, A. (2011). *Culturally responsive standards-based teaching: Classroom to community and back.* Thousand Oaks, CA: Corwin.

Sapon-Shevin, M. (2010). *Because we can change the world: A practical guide to building cooperative, inclusive classroom communities.* Thousand Oaks, CA: Corwin.

Schultz, R. (2003). Havruta: Learning in pairs. *My Jewish Learning.* Retrieved from http://www.myjewishlearning.com/article/havruta-learning-in-pairs/

Shade, B., Kelley, C., & Oberg, M. (1997). *Creating culturally responsive classrooms.* Washington, DC: American Psychological Association.

Shams, L., & Seitz, A. (2008). Benefits of multisensory learning. *Trends in Cognitive Sciences, 12*(11), 411–417.

Society for Research on Educational Effectiveness. Retrieved from https://www.sree.org/

Sousa, D. A. (2009). *How the brain influences behavior: Management strategies for every classroom.* Thousand Oaks, CA: Corwin.

Steele, D., & Cohn-Vargas, B. (2013). *Identity safe classrooms: Places to belong and learn.* Thousand Oaks, CA: Corwin.

Stiggins, R. (2006). Assessment for learning: A key to motivation & achievement. *Edge: The latest information for the education practitioner.* Retrieved from http://ati.pearson.com/downloads/edgev2n2 0.pdf

Stoyle, P. (n.d.). Storytelling benefits and tips. Retrieved from https://www.teachingenglish.org.uk/article/storytelling-benefits-tips

Strauss, K. (2006). *Tales with tails: Storytelling the wonders of the natural world.* Westport, CT: Libraries Unlimited.

Tate, M. (2010). *Worksheets won't grow dendrites: Twenty instructional strategies that engage the brain.* Thousand Oaks, CA: Corwin.

Tomlinson, C. A. (2014). *The differentiated classroom: Responding to the needs of all learners.* (2nd ed.). Alexandria, VA: ASCD.

Wright Group/McGraw Hill (2008). *Everyday mathematics, grades 2–6: Algorithms handbook.* New York, NY: McGraw Hill.

Zucker, D., & Taylor, B. (2004). Nearly everything we wish our non-Jewish supervisors had known about us as Jewish supervisees. Retrieved from http://www.davidjzucker.org/djzNEWW/index.htm

Index

A SAGE Publishing Company

Helping educators make the greatest impact

CORWIN HAS ONE MISSION: to enhance education through intentional professional learning.

We build long-term relationships with our authors, educators, clients, and associations who partner with us to develop and continuously improve the best evidence-based practices that establish and support lifelong learning.

Solutions you want. Experts you trust.
Results you need.

**AUTHOR
CONSULTING**

Author Consulting

On-site professional learning with sustainable results! Let us help you design a professional learning plan to meet the unique needs of your school or district. www.corwin.com/pd

INSTITUTES

Institutes

Corwin Institutes provide collaborative learning experiences that equip your team with tools and action plans ready for immediate implementation. www.corwin.com/institutes

ECOURSES

eCourses

Practical, flexible online professional learning designed to let you go at your own pace. www.corwin.com/ecourses

READ2EARN

Read2Earn

Did you know you can earn graduate credit for reading this book? Find out how: www.corwin.com/read2earn